# The Essence
# of the Church

## A Community Created
## by the Spirit

### Craig Van Gelder
Foreword by Richard J. Mouw

**BakerBooks**
A Division of Baker Book House Co
Grand Rapids, Michigan 49516

© 2000 by Craig Van Gelder

Published by Baker Books
a division of Baker Book House Company
P.O. Box 6287, Grand Rapids, MI 49516-6287

Fourth printing, June 2004

Printed in the United States of America

**Library of Congress Cataloging-in-Publication Data**

Van Gelder, Craig.
    The essence of the church : a community created by the Spirit / Craig Van Gelder ; foreword by Richard J. Mouw.
        p.    cm.
    Includes bibliographical references.
    ISBN 0-8010-9096-2 (pbk.)
    1. Church. 2. Church renewal—United States. I. Title.
BV600.2.V35 2000
262—dc21                                            99–055537

For information about academic books, resources for Christian leaders, and all new releases available from Baker Book House, visit our web site:

http://www.bakerbooks.com

## What lay leaders are saying about this book

"As a layman serving in leadership roles of local churches, I have felt the need for a biblical foundation upon which the Holy Spirit could build a local ministry unique to time and place yet set upon the solid foundation of Scripture. Van Gelder provides this biblical basis."

—Charles M. Bollar Jr., AIA,
president and architect,
Bollar and Associates Architects, P.C.

"A valuable contribution to discussions about the church in North America's changing cultural context. Offers challenging new insights for integrating an understanding of the biblical nature of the church with the practice of ministry. Essential reading."

—Meri MacLeod, staff director,
WorkPlace Influence, Colorado Springs, Colo.

## What pastors are saying

"A primer for rethinking the nature of the church in North America. This is better than seminary, better than journals, better than ten big books a year. Put in the hands of lay leaders, this book will create a revolution of new thinking, understanding, and learning in the church in North America."

—Rev. David Risseeuw,
Six Mile Run Reformed Church,
Reformed Church in America

"An important next step in the recovery of the church in North America. A helpful theological and biblical way for us to think about the implications of becoming missional."

—Rev. Alan Roxburgh,
West Vancouver Baptist Church,
Baptist Church of Canada

"Stands out for its willingness to draw on serious exegetical and historical study to understand the playing field of church life today. Transcends trite stereotypes and establishes a biblical missiological direction. It will be a standard reference work in this area for years to come."

—Rev. Wayne Brouwer,
Harderwyk Christian Reformed Church,
Holland, Mich.

"Most pastors I know are stressed because they are taught that they need to be successful. They say, 'If only I had the key to help my church grow or perhaps the right organizational grid or . . .' Van Gelder cuts through this false, sec-ular notion and helps church leaders formulate the right questions."

—Rev. John McLaverty,
Spring Garden Church, Baptist,
North York, Ontario

"A challenge to contemporary North American functional and organizational approaches to the church. A clear call from a biblical and missiological perspective to right imbalances within the contemporary Western church."

—Rev. Dr. Mary Lou Codman-Wilson,
associate pastor,
St. Andrew United Methodist Church,
Carol Stream, Ill.

"We need to again gain clarity on both the nature of the church and the nature of her mission. Van Gelder brings such clarity through his multidisciplinary study and effectively argues that a missiological ecclesiology can bring light instead of heat in reflecting on the nature, ministry, and organization of the church."

—Rev. Jul Medenblik,
New Life Church, Christian Reformed Church,
New Lenox, Ill.

"The people of God have too long been frozen out of their rightful calling as the most exhilarating project God has conceived in our day and age. Practitioners of ministry will be well served by this reasoned and well-crafted primer on the central calling of our faith."

—Rev. Doug Ward,
Kanata Baptist Church, Kanata, Ontario

"Offers church leaders hope by showing how the church of Jesus Christ has always been and will continue to be built through the ministry of the Holy Spirit. As a church planter, it left me hungering to see how the Spirit will organize our newly emerging congregation into a visible missional community."

—Rev. Ken Nydam, New Life Community
Church, Grand Junction, Colo.

## What denominational staff are saying

"Stimulating and practical reading for the pastor, lay person, or church executive who wants to think deeply about the biblical, theological, and cultural call for God's people to fulfill Christ's mission on earth."

—Rev. Stan Wood, new church development,
Colombia Theological Seminary

"An important statement on the missional nature of the church within the context of North America. Challenges the how-to books that skip the discussion of what the church is and go directly to what the church should do and how it should organize."

—Rev. Lois Barrett, executive secretary,
Commission on Home Ministries,
General Conference Mennonite Church

"Most church leaders acknowledge that the church needs to change. This book helps us build the foundation for a sound missiological ecclesiology so we may become re-engaged in God's mission among us."

—Rev. James H. Furr, senior church consultant,
Union Baptist Association,
Houston, Tex., Southern Baptist Convention

"Calls us to respond to the North American context in which the church finds itself as fully in a 'missionary situation.' Helps us discern the missiological interrelationships of the church's nature, ministry, and organization as it fulfills God's call to mission in a post-Christian world."

—Rev. Eugene Heideman,
former secretary for program,
Reformed Church in America

"This fine introduction to thinking about the church helps us understand how biblical, historical, and contextual forces shape the church's self-understanding. A danger to the status quo and foundational for reshaping the church."

—Rev. Dirk Hart, minister of evangelism,
Christian Reformed Church in North America

"An excellent history of ecclesiology. Van Gelder helps us see the changing assumptions of church organization through the years. An important reflection on the missional nature of the church. Every missiologist should read it."

—Rev. Robert J. Scudieri, area secretary for
North America, Lutheran Church Missouri Synod

## What professors of theology are saying

"One of the few works I have encountered that offers a sustained reflection on the church's essential and constitutive missionary nature. A genuine breakthrough in ecclesiology."

—Dr. Steve Bevans,
professor of doctrinal theology,
Catholic Theological Union

"Wrestles in a fresh way with the ancient problem of the Christian church: that it is both spiritual and social, both the work of the Holy Spirit and a human organization working in society. All who care about the way the promise of God for the world expresses itself in human community and human witness will be helped by his study."

—Dr. Charles C. West,
professor of Christian ethics emeritus,
Princeton Theological Seminary,
Presbyterian Church (U.S.A.)

## What professors of mission are saying

"Eureka!!—a book which officiates the long-awaited wedding of ecclesiology and missiology. Behold, a missiological ecclesiology! What Van Gelder has joined together, let no theologian put asunder!"

—Dr. Justice C. Anderson,
former professor of missions,
Southwestern Baptist Theological Seminary

"A constructive and stimulating contribution to the growing conversation about the missionary vocation of the church in North America. Introduces perspectives into the conversation that will assist in the movement of the church towards its missional vocation."

—Dr. Darrell L. Guder,
professor of evangelism and church growth,
Columbia Theological Seminary,
Presbyterian Church (U.S.A.)

## What mission organization leaders are saying

"When facing difficult decisions, pastors and lay leaders need help from many places at once, such as the Bible, theology, management, missiology, and sociology. Van Gelder brings together insights from these fields and presents them in ways that are both readable and practical."

—Rev. James M. Phillips, former assistant
director, Overseas Mission Study Center

"At a time when church leaders are more inclined to seek after the latest ministry trend than to discern the Spirit's leading, Van Gelder is a direction setter. Affirming the essential missionary nature of the church, this book will keep the church on course in the twenty-first century."

—Don Posterski, World Vision Canada

# Contents

to
##  Barbara,

who has continued to be a loving wife
and faithful friend through twenty-seven years together,
and who has always encouraged me
to put my thoughts into writing

# Foreword

North America is a mission field where effective ministry requires skills in cross-cultural communication. Anyone who doubts this needs only spend a little time watching MTV or listening to call-in radio programs or reading *People* magazine.

Some say that the missionary context is a new one for the Christian community in North America. There was a time, they insist, when our culture was more Christian. But things have changed. Pluralism and new paganism have come to dominate the scene. So today we need to think more missiologically than we did in the past.

Others argue that we are finally becoming aware of a long-standing reality. Past generations of North American Christians were deceived by the "Christendom" idea. What they thought of as the influence of the gospel on their cultural surroundings was nothing more than a superficial religiosity. Today the illusion of a "Christian culture" can no longer be sustained, and not just because of the obvious fact of the mosques and temples being built by new immigrant groups. Many members of today's unreached people groups have the blood of Puritan ancestors flowing through their veins.

The argument is an interesting one for scholars, and there are important issues at stake. But when we focus on the practical questions of what it means to be the church in our present context, there is little about which to argue. However we understand our past, today's missionary mandate is clear. In this book, Craig Van Gelder provides wise and necessary guidance to all of us who care deeply about how the church can minister effectively to a culture that desperately needs to experience the transforming power of the gospel of Jesus Christ.

Van Gelder has given us an important "bridge" book. For starters, he sensitively bridges past and present. This is one reason why I find his treatment of the issues so helpful. Like him, I am not very impressed by those thinkers who urge us to scrap all previous ecclesiological formulations and confront contemporary challenges with a clean slate. Van Gelder is convinced that much wisdom can be found in past discussions of the nature of the church and its ministries and structures. Yet he also knows that those voices from the past have not spoken the final word about what God wants the church to be and do.

Van Gelder also demonstrates much skill in bridging theory and practice. He has obviously done his homework in recent organizational theory, management studies, and cultural analysis—to say nothing of the various traditions and branches of classical theology. But while his discussion is informed by careful scholarship, the focus is on the very real practical challenges that are facing the church in contemporary North America.

Most important is the bridging he sets forth in this fine book that shows the intimate connections between ecclesiology and missiology. Van Gelder is very aware of the reductionisms often associated with simple ecclesiological formulas: "the church is mission," "the church is radical community," "the church is the depository of divine truth." With sensitivity to the richness of the biblical message, he makes it clear that the church cannot be what God wants it to be without doing what God calls it to do—and vice versa!

This is an important book for present-day missionaries—which is to say that it should be required reading for all who want the church to be faithful to the cause of the gospel in our present cultural context.

Richard J. Mouw, president
Fuller Theological Seminary

# Preface

This book is about the church. While there is much literature already available on this topic, this book seeks to offer the reader a fresh perspective. My approach reflects my journey over the past three decades. I have incorporated into the text insights gained from years spent as a parachurch campus worker, a graduate student, a church consultant, an ordained minister, and a seminary professor.

In writing this book, I have four goals. The first is to *translate available scholarship and research* into an applied perspective for ministry. While I hope professional academics will find this volume helpful, it is intended primarily for pastors and church leaders as a primer on thinking deeply, yet practically, about the church. In my experience as a church consultant for over two decades, I have found that most pastors and church leaders appreciate good scholarship, but they also live in a day-to-day world where scholarship, to be helpful, must be translated into an applied perspective.

This book is intended to serve such persons in grounding their ministries in sound biblical, theological, and theoretical perspectives. It draws carefully on the excellent existing scholarship and research on the church within a variety of disciplines. But it presents these materials in a readable format from an applied perspective. For the interested reader, I have referenced in the endnotes the more technical aspects of the related discussions.

My second goal is to *integrate diverse perspectives* from a variety of disciplines, including: mission theology, the doctrine of the church, organizational development, management studies, cultural analysis, leadership development, and spiritual formation. This commitment is shaped largely by my experience as a graduate student when I worked on two Ph.D. programs at the same time—one in mission theology and practice at Southwestern Baptist Theological Seminary, the other in urban administration at the University of Texas at Arlington. Through this experience, I discovered the benefits of having to think through the interrelationship of diverse perspectives presented within the fields of theology and the social sciences. At some points, these perspectives were complementary, but at times they were in conflict. During this time I became convinced of the value of applying my theological framework to the perspectives offered by the social sciences.

Many fields of study, both within theology and the social sciences, are now providing us with helpful insights on the church. But the insights and perspectives of one field of study are often left unrelated to those offered by other disciplines. While not trying to be exhaustive, this work does attempt to integrate insights and perspectives from diverse disciplines as they relate to how we view the church.

My third goal for this book is to *focus on the church within the context of North America*. At Luther Seminary where I hold the position of Professor of Congregational Mission and at Calvin Theological Seminary where I served in a similar role for ten years as Professor of Domestic Missiology, my responsibility has been to focus attention on the life and ministry of the North American church from the perspective of God's mission in the world. As Richard Mouw points out in his foreword, there is a growing awareness that we need to think of North America as a mission field. Approaching the church in North America from a mission perspective opens up some critical issues.

The church must always seek to be relevant within its specific cultural context. Within North America over the past several centuries, churches have worked hard to be relevant to a variety of contexts. While many aspects of these expressions of the church can be viewed as strengths, discernment must also be used in critiquing how the gospel relates to specific contexts.

There is always the danger that elements of the culture will compromise the biblical nature of the church and its ministry. While the primary focus throughout this volume is on biblical and theological perspectives, these will be explored in terms of how they impact our understanding of the church within the specific context of North America.

My fourth goal is for this book to *work from an understanding of the Triune God*—Father, Son, and Spirit—as being central to our understanding of the church. This commitment is shaped largely by my own pilgrimage in Christian ministry. I was initially influenced by the evangelical passions of a parachurch campus ministry that emphasized a cross-centered gospel that calls for obedience to the Great Commission as the primary task of all Christians. Later, receiving a seminary education at Reformed Theological Seminary helped me to relate the cross to God's purposes within creation and to God's future intentions for the new heaven and new earth. In the last decade, these insights have matured into a more honest biblical and experiential reckoning with the power of the gospel as it confronts, in the name of Jesus through the work of the Spirit, "the principalities and powers" (Eph. 6:12) in our world.

This journey is summed up in many ways in the recent renewed emphasis on understanding the life and ministry of the church from the perspective of God as a trinity. A trinitarian understanding is now the common starting point for thinking about God's people in the world, about the church, and about how the church participates in God's mission in the world. Because of the applied emphasis of this book, particular attention is focused on the Spirit as that person of the Trinity sent to carry out God's redemptive purposes in the world, especially as the Spirit relates to God's mission in the world through the church. To develop a biblical perspective on the church, we must have a biblical perspective on the life and ministry of the Spirit. My prayer is that a better understanding of these issues will help the church better fulfill its role in God's redemptive purposes in our world.

Over the years, many friends have greatly helped me clarify and sharpen the thoughts that appear in this book. I express my profound gratitude to all of them for their contributions. In particular, however, I want to thank the many colleagues who agreed to read a draft of this manuscript and provide helpful critique and suggestions for improving the argument. While in no way holding them responsible for what is presented here, I want all to know how greatly I was served by their contributions. These colleagues, in addition to Richard Mouw, who so graciously provided the foreword, include Justice C. Anderson, Lois Barrett, Steve Bevans, Charles M. Bollar, Wayne Brouwer, Mary Lou Codman-Wilson, James Furr, Darrell L. Guder, Dirk Hart, Eugene Heideman, Meri MacLeod, John McLaverty, Jul Medenblik, Ken Nydam, James M. Phillips, Don Posterski, David Risseeuw, Alan Roxburgh, Robert J. Scudieri, Doug Ward, Charles C. West, and Stan Wood.

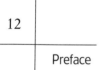

Preface

# ONE

# Rediscovering the Church in the Twenty-First Century

It was another typical Sunday morning in Springdale,[1] a fairly typical suburb of twenty-five thousand located on the fringes of a city of a half million. Twenty-six churches served the residents of Springdale and the surrounding area. Most had been started as congregations of various denominations during the baby boom years of the 1950s and 1960s, but several independent community churches had sprung up in recent years. In addition, two churches had recently been formed to serve the growing number of middle-class African-American and Hispanic residents who over the past two decades had grown to make up fifteen percent of the community's population. As on every other Sunday morning, many of Springdale's residents were getting ready for church.

Jane was reflecting on how much she enjoyed attending worship in her church with its dignified service. She especially enjoyed the peaceful, quiet atmosphere of the building with its refined architecture.

Bill was thinking about all the controversy that had resulted from his church's recent decision to change the morning service from 11:00 to 9:00.

Mary was still feeling troubled about her church's position on social issues and frustrated by all the time it took the church to decide things. These problems seemed to be getting in the way of unity in her congregation.

Greg had promised to go to church with his wife and kids, so he was going with her, but he reminded her that he felt his real church was the Thursday morning Bible study he attended with other businessmen.

Sarah, a lifelong member of the Catholic Church, wondered about the Protestant churches many of her friends attended and wished they would join her at least once to experience her church.

Jim was still thinking about the controversy that had surfaced at last week's council meeting over the pastor's authority in relation to the council's authority. As a businessman he wondered why his church was structured in such a seemingly inefficient way.

Reverend Olson was putting the final touches on his communion message that morning as he reflected on why Word and Sacrament are so important, and how to convey this one more time in a fresh way.

## Church

The word *church* carries many meanings. This particular morning the residents of Springdale gave it seven different meanings: a building, an event, a policy body, a relational group, an institutionalized denomination, an organizational style, and the practice of affirming correct confessional criteria. Each of these meanings carries some truth about what we understand the church to be in North America. They also convey something of the challenge we face in understanding the church in this setting.

What exactly is the church? Certainly it is more than a physical structure. It is more than a programmed event that we attend a certain time each week. It is more than a set of policy choices that define how resources are allocated, and more than one's personal relationships with other believers. The church is more than a historical denomination, more than a particular type of organizational structure, and more than a set of communally affirmed confessional beliefs.

The church exists in relation to all these meanings. But it is more than any one of them, and, in fact, more than all of them combined. When we encounter the church, we move into spiritual territory that occupies earthly terrain. We encounter the living God in the midst of our humanity. We encounter the Spirit of God dwelling in the midst of a people who are created and formed into a unique community. As these communities study the Bible, examine their history, and explore their settings, they take on particular names, styles, structures, and behaviors—and they become diverse.

## Church in the North American Context

There is certainly an abundance of churches in North America, and it is clear that they are deeply woven into the national stories of both the United States and Canada. They are so much a part of the landscape that we tend to take them for granted. The profile of the churches serving the suburb of Springdale is typical of communities across North America. Their variety and diversity is outlined in figure 1.[2]

Such variety! Churches come with a wide array of names and labels. But we need to recognize that they serve as important social institutions providing a point of religious identity for millions of North Americans.[3]

Such numbers! In the U.S. alone, we find over 300,000 congregations, most of which are linked within several hundred denominations.[4] Today in North America, the diversity of the church at times may cause us to lose sight of its uniqueness as the creation of the Spirit. We are forced to try to make sense of a complex array of *denominations, missional structures,* and *local congregations* that all claim to be part of the Christian movement. To appreciate this complexity, it is helpful to examine these three forms more closely.

### Denominations

Denominations are the way most persons in North America encounter the institutional character of the church. This form of church is a fairly recent invention in church history, only about two centuries old.[5] The denomination found fertile soil within the emerging colonies and territories of what later

## Figure 1

## Churches in Springdale

| Denomination | Number Churches | Total Adherents |
|---|---|---|
| AME Zion | 1* | 225 |
| American Baptist USA | 3 | 875 |
| Assembly of God | 1 | 450 |
| Catholic—Latin | 2 | 1,250 |
| Christian Churches and Churches of Christ | 1 | 275 |
| Christian Missionary Alliance | 1 | 175 |
| Church of Jesus Christ of Latter-Day Saints | 1 | 450 |
| Episcopal | 2 | 650 |
| Evangelical Lutheran Church in America | 2 | 770 |
| Lutheran Church— Missouri Synod | 1 | 328 |
| Pentecostal Holiness | 1 | 231 |
| Presbyterian Church (USA) | 2 | 490 |
| Reformed Church in America | 1 | 260 |
| Southern Baptist Convention | 1 | 175 |
| United Church of Christ | 1 | 220 |
| United Methodist Church | 3** | 920 |
| Faith Community (independent) | 1 | 775 |
| Fellowship Community (independent) | 1 | 1,100 |
| **Totals** | **26** | **9,619** |

*This African-American church recently relocated from an older neighborhood and purchased a Nazarene building where they now worship. About half of their members live in the Springdale community and half drive from other areas.

**One of these UMC churches is a new congregation serving the growing number of Hispanic residents in the community, although some of these residents attend the Catholic churches.

Rediscovering the Church in the Twenty-First Century

became the United States and Canada. While about fifty denominations account for the vast majority of the Christian population in these two nations, several hundred denominations dot the landscape. This form of the church, though recent in history, has been dynamic in structure. It has gone through at least five identifiable phases of growth and development.[6]

## Historical Development of Denominations

*Phase 1: Ethnic-Voluntarism Denomination, 1600–1800.* This denominational type emerged in the early seventeenth to late eighteenth centuries and functioned as a coalition of ethnic immigrant churches of European parentage.

*Phase 2: The Purposive-Missionary Denomination, 1800–1850.* During the first half of the nineteenth century, this denominational type was formed as a national organizational structure responsible to introduce new churches into the expanding frontier.

*Phase 3: The Churchly Denomination, 1850–1900.* During the last half of the nineteenth century, denominations transitioned to this type as they built extensive institutional systems to serve the needs of their members.

*Phase 4: The Corporate Denomination, 1900–1965.* During the first half of the twentieth century, denominations created multiple agencies within an extensive bureaucratic hierarchy to manage the ministry of member churches.

*Phase 5: The Regulatory Denomination, 1965 to present.* In the last half of the twentieth century, a type of denomination has emerged that increasingly uses rules and policies to secure compliance from member churches.

How are we to understand this complexity of denominational development? Should we think of denominations primarily in theological, historical, sociological, or organizational terms, or in all of these ways?[7] What is clear is that denominations must be reckoned with if we are to make sense of the church in North America. This represents one of the primary challenges in try-

17

ing to recover biblical and theological foundations for understanding the church.

## Missional Structures

A second way we encounter the church is in a variety of missional structures. Some of these exist within denominations as connectional structures (often referred to as ecclesiastical structures). We find, for example, dioceses for Roman Catholics, conferences for United Methodists, districts for the Lutheran Church-Missouri Synod, presbyteries for Presbyterians (USA), classes for the Reformed Church in America, associations for Southern Baptists, and so forth. The purpose of these ecclesiastical structures is to bring a common order and shared life to the various member congregations. Other missional structures within denominations exist as agencies to carry out various aspects of denominational ministry.[8] Thus we find home mission agencies, foreign mission agencies, educational agencies, service agencies, justice agencies, publishing agencies, and more.

In addition to these denominational structures and agencies, a wide variety of missional structures exist independent of churches. These organizational forms have been given such names as parachurch organizations, faith missions, mission societies, and Christian movements. In Springdale, residents are involved in all the following independent Christian organizations.

### Independent Missional Structures in Springdale

- Young Life group at the local high school
- Businessmen involved in an area chapter of Christian Business Men's Committee
- Groups of men meeting in churches in relation to Promise Keepers
- Numerous women involved in Bible Study Fellowship
- Several families supporting staff working with Campus Crusade for Christ

- A staff member who works for Child Evangelism Fellowship
- Several doctors who volunteer time with the Luke Society

Each such organization usually exists to carry out some specialized ministry.[9] Each sees its ministry as being beyond the capacity of local congregations to carry out, or as being needed to reach beyond the provincial character of denominational systems.

## Local Congregations

Another form in which we encounter the church, and perhaps the most basic way, is in local congregations. This familiar expression of the church has firm biblical foundations, but its development in North America has been diverse. Congregations represent various phases of historical growth that correspond to the development of denominations outlined above. Thus, we find ethnic-village congregations, purposive-village congregations, institutional congregations, organizational congregations, and lifestyle congregations, all within the broader system of denominations.[10]

Understanding a particular congregation is a complex task. One must take into account the historical developments surrounding it, but a host of other factors must also be given careful attention. These include such internal factors as membership size, ministry style, program model, organizational structure, volunteer involvement, the physical plant, and financial resources. They also include such external factors as location, traffic patterns, population characteristics, and community needs.[11] Local congregations are complex creations of the Spirit that require leaders to exercise sophisticated management and organizational skills to give direction to the work of the Spirit in their midst.

These organizational forms—denominations, missional structures, and local congregations—raise some basic questions. Where did they come from? How do they express biblical foundations and historical legitimacy as the church? What is their purpose? What is their future? Such questions are academically interesting, but they are also important for church leaders today for practical reasons. Churches are confronted by the complexities of modern life and the emerging postmodern culture,[12] and most are finding it difficult to define their role in the changing North American context. Many of these structures are struggling to redefine their very reason for existence.

There are different responses to this challenge, many of which draw on current practices in the social sciences. One management practice many church leaders are using is clarifying values, defining the mission, and focusing a vision as a response to a changing context and shifting culture. Other leaders are focusing on reshaping existing structures to increase organizational effectiveness. These are important matters to address in the life and ministry of the church, but the use of such management practices and organizational skills has often become part of the problem. We have been inundated over the past several decades with approaches that call for better management and more effective organization within the church. These include the church renewal movement of the 1960s and 1970s, the church growth movement of the 1970s and 1980s, and the church effectiveness movement of the 1980s and 1990s.[13] As helpful as many of these emphases have been, they have often failed to grapple with deeper realities about the church.

## The Church Is the Solution: A Functional Approach

An example of how some of these deeper realities have been missed can be found in the recent effectiveness literature. Here we find an emphasis on making the ministry of the church responsive to a changing context. This literature usually emphasizes the importance of rediscovering the biblical ministry of the church and using these insights to make the ministry of the church more relevant to today's world. This approach proceeds from what might be described as a functional view of the church, one that defines the church primarily in terms of what it does. Reshaping a church's ministry is seen as the solution for responding to a new or changed ministry context. The current effectiveness literature describes a variety of such functional approaches for defining the church and its ministry.[14]

## Current Examples of Functional Approaches

- *Seeker-Sensitive Church.* Emphasizes conducting worship services shaped for evangelism of unchurched persons
- *Purpose-Driven Church.* Emphasizes defining clearly the purpose of the church around core functions and building intentional processes of discipling
- *Small-Group Church.* Emphasizes making small groups the critical infrastructure for church life in complement with gathered celebrative worship
- *User-Friendly Church.* Emphasizes developing processes around key biblical principles that attract people into high-commitment communities
- *Seven-Day-a-Week Church.* Emphasizes expanding group-based, weekday ministries as multiple points of entry into the life of the church
- *Church for the 21st Century.* Emphasizes developing a church as a major anchor of ministry that can specialize in a variety of niche markets

Many of the books proposing such approaches provide keen insights into developing aspects of the church's ministry. They also provide helpful perspective on adapting ministry to respond to our current culture. All of these approaches, however, tend to treat the church in functional terms. That is, they view the church primarily in terms of what churches do. "Doing" the church's ministry is absolutely essential to a full view of the church. But such a functional approach to defining the church leaves unaddressed some basic questions about the nature of the church.

21

# The Church Is the Problem:
## An Organizational Approach

There is also a current literature that focuses on the organizational structure of the church, especially in relation to churches encountering changing contexts. Here the focus is on diagnosing weaknesses in the organizational life of the church and applying these insights to the task of reinvigorating ministry. Perspectives from the organizational and managerial sciences are usually incorporated into this restructuring work. This organizational view defines the church in terms of its structures, procedures, and decision-making processes. The emphasis is on solving problems in the church's organizational life to improve its ministry. Recent examples in the literature of such organizational approaches include the following.[15]

## Recent Examples of Organizational Approaches

- *Denominational Cultures.* An analysis and classification of denominations based upon their theological views and social attitudes, along with changes in these patterns over time
- *Congregational Studies.* The use of theories and tools from the social sciences to evaluate and explain contextual and institutional characteristics of congregations
- *Church Growth and Decline.* Measuring and evaluating patterns of growth and decline within congregations and denominational systems
- *Reinventing Denominations.* An application to denominational systems of the current organizational approaches to reengineering institutional structures
- *Quality Evaluation.* An application to the organizational life of churches of the current literature on total quality management and outcome-based evaluation

- *Systems Management.* Use of a systems approach from organizational theory to understand and improve the management of church organizations

Many of the books taking such approaches provide helpful insights into understanding the organizational dynamics of churches, and most suggest ways in which church systems and structures might be renewed for ministry. All of these approaches tend to treat the church in sociological or organizational terms. They develop their view of the church primarily in terms of the structures that make up the organizational life of churches. An understanding of the church's structural character is essential to a full view of the church, but this approach also leaves unaddressed some basic questions about the church's nature.

## The Church Is

Failing to understand the nature of the church can lead to a number of problems. Defining the church functionally—in terms of what it does—can shift our perspective away from understanding the church as a unique community of God's people. In place of this, the church tends to become a series of ministry functions such as worship, education, service, and witness. Defining the church organizationally—in terms of its structures—can shift our perspective away from the spiritual reality of the church as a social community. The church becomes a patterned set of human behaviors to be structured and managed. These approaches reduce the church to a set of ministries administered through management skills to maintain effectiveness, or to an organization designed to accomplish certain goals. These functional and organizational approaches can seduce leaders into placing too much confidence in their managerial skills or in their use of organizational techniques.

A recent article in *The Atlantic Monthly* focused national attention on getting ready for the "next" church where the key to success is outlined in terms of functional ministry that is culturally relevant and organizationally sound.[16] It is my conviction that we need to move beyond trying to find the "next" church that will help us be successful one more time. We need to rediscover something more basic about what it means *to be* the church.

Functional and organizational approaches to understanding the church rely heavily on the social sciences. While insights from the social sciences can be helpful, these perspectives tend to give primary emphasis to the human dimensions of church life. The church is not just another human organization that happens to have a different mandate for its life and ministry. The church is about human behavior that is being transformed through God's redeeming power, and about patterns of life that reflect redemptive purposes. Use of the social sciences must be kept in perspective within a theological framework and must be placed in relationship to God's redemptive presence in the church. Therefore, it is critical that we consider the *nature* of the church before proceeding to define its *ministry* and *organization*. To do so, we must start from a theological perspective.

A number of observers, especially those dealing with the relationship between gospel and culture, are pointing out that something more fundamental is going on in today's discussion about the church.[17] The issue is not so much our ability to focus the ministry of the church, or our ability to analyze and renew existing church structures. The more basic issue we face is the very way we think about the church. The critical question is, What is the church? To answer this question, we must understand that the church's nature is unique, and that this unique nature is the result of the work of God's Spirit in the world. Understanding this unique nature provides the necessary perspective for addressing the ministry and organization of the church.

## The Church Is Created by the Spirit

The church is more than what meets the eye. It is more than a set of well-managed ministry functions. It is more than another human organization. The church lives in the world as a human enterprise, but it is also the called and redeemed people of God. It is a people of God who are created by the Spirit to live as a missionary community. As such, the church is both a social organization and a spiritual community. (Note that the word "social," as it is used here and throughout the rest of this book, refers to a "human community of persons in relationship with one another.")

There is a duality within the church's nature which we must understand if we are to address properly the ministry and organization of the church.[18] The church is God's personal presence in the world through the Spirit. This makes the church, as a spiritual community, unique. The church also exists as a social reality with human behaviors organized within human structures. But this human behavior, through the redemptive work of God, is empowered by the Spirit. This is the duality inherent in the church's nature.

Most Christians in North America have a distorted picture of church. We have a distorted understanding of the church's nature—its unique character as a community of God's people. We also have a distorted understanding of the church's ministry—its full expression of living as a community under God's reign. And we have a distorted understanding of the church's organization—how it is to structure itself to carry out its ministry consistent with its nature. We need to fundamentally rethink our understanding of the church's nature, ministry, and organization in our North American context.

We can best begin this rethinking by drawing on the insights of two distinct but complementary theological disciplines that seek to understand the life and ministry of the church. One discipline is the field of missiology—the study of mission. The other is the field of ecclesiology—the study of the church.

*Missiology: The Study of Mission.* This field of theological study focuses on how to proclaim the gospel and grow the church in different cultural contexts. Attention is given to such matters as mission theology, world religions, cross-cultural communication, training missionaries, mission methods, church planting, and evangelism. All of this is framed in light of the mission of the Triune God in the world.

*Ecclesiology: The Study of the Church.* This field of theological study focuses on understanding the church in terms of its nature, ministry, and organization. Attention is given to such matters as biblical and theological foundations, historical ecclesiologies (different views of the church in different periods of time), and church polity (how different churches have been organized). All of this is related to God's redemptive purposes in the world.

There are many natural points of overlap within these two theological disciplines, but for a variety of reasons, they have developed separately in North America. This is true both in the ministry of congregations and in the training offered by theological seminaries. Discovering the common ground between these disciplines and identifying their relationship is critical to the task of rethinking the church in North America. We turn to this task in the next chapter.

# A Missional Understanding of the Church

Bill, Greg, and Jim were having their regular Monday morning cup of coffee at the local Starbuck's in Springdale. The conversation turned to what was going on in their local congregations.

Bill had just been appointed to the evangelism committee of Wesley United Methodist. This had occurred after he spoke up at the yearly congregational meeting saying his church needed to be more concerned about evangelism. It was not clear to Bill how this committee's work related to the rest of the ministry of the church. Were committee members supposed to knock on doors? Or were they to train other church members to do evangelism?

Greg said that he had tried for years to do evangelism through his local church, Springdale Presbyterian (USA), but had eventually given up. He and others who had a burden in this area had introduced a training program called Evangelism Explosion and had succeeded in mobilizing about twenty members for a while. But after about two years, it became evident that the church didn't know how to enfold the several persons who had come to faith through their work. In frustration, Greg had joined the Christian Business Men's Committee (CBMC) where he and others regularly saw friends coming to faith in Christ. He had noticed, though, that most of these men never developed a strong association with a local church; their involvement in CBMC seemed to be enough to meet their spiritual needs.

Jim mentioned that he was serving on the missions committee of his church, Woodlawn Southern Baptist. Over

30 percent of the total church revenues went yearly to foreign missions. Most of this money was raised at the annual weeklong Missions festival. His committee was busy planning this year's festival and was adding to the normal agenda of missionary speakers some workers who represented Christian service organizations in the local urban area. The theme for this year's event was "Across the Sea—Across the Street." They were hoping to mobilize more of their members to go beyond giving their dollars to overseas missions by getting personally involved in local missions work.

This conversation reflects the way most Christians in North America understand the concepts of missions and evangelism. Missions is usually understood as something churches support that takes place somewhere else through specially trained professionals known as missionaries. Evangelism is often seen as something a few persons do in a local congregation through a committee, or as one of the programs of the church, or as something done in and through a parachurch organization like CBMC.

There are two fundamental problems with such understandings. First, they fail to relate missions and evangelism adequately to the larger framework of the mission of God. And second, because of this, they fail to recognize the relationship between the life and ministry of the church and God's mission in the world.

## Relating Mission to an Understanding of the Church

The concepts of church and mission are two important ways of thinking about God's work in the world. The development of our understanding of the *church* has a long history. It starts on the pages of the New Testament and continues through the centuries as the church develops various definitions of its life and ministry in the world. These views, or self-understandings of the church, are known as ecclesiologies. An *ecclesiology* is a summary of what the church, working within a particular historical context, believes the Bible to teach about the character and purpose of the church in relation to that setting.

The concept of *mission* has a different heritage. Its role in the New Testament church is clear from the story of the expansion of the Christian movement in the first-century world. Mission activity also took place through the church during different periods of the church's history as the Christian movement spread into new areas. However, a specialized meaning became associated with this concept during the past two hundred years. This period witnessed the rise of the modern missions movement, with scores of mission societies coming into existence that worked through or alongside the churches in the West. Most were designed to carry the message of the gospel to other places in the world, but many were also started to extend the work of the church at home. William Carey articulated this approach in his famous treatise in 1792. He said that missions is a specialized function grounded primarily in the biblical mandate that Christians are personally responsible to obey the Great Commission.[1] Many churches in North America hold to this view today, including many of those in Springdale.

The churches in North America formed many agencies to carry out specialized missions throughout the world. This work became known as world missions and is associated with such concepts as world evangelization, church planting, and cross-cultural ministry. North American churches also engaged in extensive missions work within their own countries. This became known as home missions and became associated with such concepts as revivals, crusades, church extension, evangelism programs, and ministry to specialized populations.

All of these efforts, both abroad and at home, are defined by the term *missions*. In this view, missions work is one among several essential tasks of the church. Congregations often debate over how to prioritize these tasks: Should priority be given to ministry to members or to evangelism? How much of our budget do we send overseas? How much do we keep at home?

In world missions, the church delegates its work to specially called and trained persons known as foreign missionaries. When these missionaries cross salt water, they and their work often take on "sacredness." For missions work in North America, these specially trained persons are known as home missionaries. They usually work with specialized subpopulations such as Native Americans, recent immigrants, or inner-city residents, where it is common for them to start what are usually referred to as "mission churches" among these groups.[2] Within local churches, this view of missions as a specialized task is usually practiced as evangelism. The approaches taken include evangelism committees, programmed gospel presentations, special training for evangelism, and above all, an expectation that each individual Christian should engage in personal evangelism. This concept is often popularized in slogans like "each one reach one."[3]

## Missions As a Function

It is important to distinguish between the terms *mission* and *missions.* That little *s* can lead to significant misunderstandings.[4] In common usage, the term *missions* describes the structures and activities that grew up during the modern missions movement. These structures carry out a critical aspect of the ministry of the church and are woven into its organizational life. They are important, but they must also be placed in proper perspective.

These activities and structures are sometimes also referred to in the singular as the "mission of the church" or the "church's mission." This use of the term *mission,* just like the plural form *missions,* refers to one of many functions of the church. Understanding missions or mission as a functional task of the church only partially addresses the issue of mission.

## Mission As Inherent in the Church's Nature

Another understanding of mission has entered the discussion in recent decades. This view considers mission to be inherent within the very nature of the church. It starts with the belief that the Triune God is a missionary God. God's missionary character is expressed, first of all, in the work of creation. God formed

A Missional Understanding of the Church

a world in which the crowning touch, human beings, became participants in creation's full development. After the fall, God's missionary character is again expressed in the work of redemption. God sent Jesus into the world to restore right relationship with all that was lost in the fall. God's missionary character is also expressed in the work of consummation. God will act in history to bring all creation to a new fullness and to completion.

From this perspective, the church, as the people of God in the world, is inherently a missionary church. It is to participate fully in the Son's redemptive work as the Spirit creates, leads, and teaches the church to live as the distinctive people of God. With this understanding, mission shifts from naming a *function* of the church to describing its essential *nature*. This has direct implications for all aspects of the church's ministry. It shifts our understanding of both missiology and ecclesiology. It reshapes our understanding of the nature, ministry, and organization of the church.

According to this view, church and mission are not two distinct entities. They speak about the same reality. Whenever church and mission are presented as distinct entities, we tend to end up with dichotomies between ministry functions and competition among organizational structures.[5]

Church and mission need to be merged into a common concept. Ecclesiology and missiology are not separate theological disciplines, but are, in fact, interrelated and complementary. They start at the same point, with the Triune God in mission to all of creation. They speak of the same reality—the church is to participate fully in God's mission to all of creation. We need to integrate our understanding of church and mission. We need to develop a missiological ecclesiology.

## A Missiological Ecclesiology

Missiology and ecclesiology share much in common in their understanding of God's work in the world. Many churches in the two-thirds world have worked to integrate these perspectives. But for the most part, in North America these disciplines still function separately with each practicing its own way of framing the other. Some solutions have been tried, but most have been unbalanced.[6]

Those who start with a theology of the church and proceed to mission usually make mission a functional task of the church. This is especially true of churches influenced by the modern missions movement. Within this movement, the church is viewed in institutional terms, with mission being one of several tasks the church undertakes on God's behalf.

Those who start with a theology of mission and proceed to the church usually approach the church as something developed through the work of missionaries. Winning lost persons and mobilizing the church become the top priorities. This perspective often fails to incorporate an adequate understanding of the historical existence of the institutional church.

Understanding the church as being missionary by nature represents a more holistic way of thinking about mission. In this view, the Spirit-created church lives as the very body of Christ in the world. Its existence declares that the full power of God's redemptive work is already active in the world through the Spirit. It lives as a demonstration that heaven has already begun for God's people. This Spirit-led community possesses all the power of God's presence, even while it awaits the final judgment of evil that will lead to the creation of the new heavens and new earth.

We in North America need to thoroughly work this perspective into our understanding of the church's nature, ministry, and organizational life. This view of the church, best described as a missiological ecclesiology, is the focus of this book.

## Contributions from Missiology and Ecclesiology

In recent years, significant developments in both missiology and ecclesiology have led to a better understanding that mission and church address the same reality.

## Developments in Missiology

The formal discipline of missiology emerged within seminary education in the late nineteenth century.[7] Its development was related to the vast expansion of the modern missions movement, and it primarily saw missions as a task of the church. A theology of mission within the modern missions movement tended to start with the Great Commission and the call for personal obedience to carry this out by evangelizing "the heathen" or "the nations."[8]

During the past fifty years, the discipline of missiology has undergone a significant shift from defining missions as a task of the church to understanding mission as an inherent aspect of the nature of the church. In fact, even the concept of a "theology of mission" is being replaced, in light of this shift, by an understanding that all theology is inherently "mission theology."[9]

Mission theology links the missionary nature of the church to an understanding of the mission of the Triune God. The understanding of the Triune God in mission to all of creation was proposed under the title of *Missio Dei* by Wilhelm Anderson in 1952 at the meeting of the International Missionary Council (IMC) at Willingen, Germany.[10] During the 1960s, this view was reinforced by developments in biblical theology regarding the kingdom of God as the key message announced by Jesus in his person and work. These studies identified the "already" character of the kingdom of God as being related to the presence of God's Spirit in the world.[11] They identified the "not yet" aspect of this kingdom as a waiting for the final consummation and judgment of evil. The redemptive reign of God as inaugurated by Jesus was integrated with an understanding of the Triune God seeking to redeem all of creation. The mission of God in all of creation was being carried out through the church in the power of the Spirit. This viewpoint has now become a shared starting point for various streams of missiology.

Roman Catholics began to speak and write from this perspective in conjunction with documents formulated by Vatican II in the early 1960s and through a series of conferences in Latin America in the 1960s and 1970s.[12] This was reinforced by

A Missional Understanding of the Church

a document issued by Pope Paul VI in the mid-1970s.[13] Ecumenicals began to speak and write from this perspective in connection with the merger of the IMC into the World Council of Churches (WCC) in 1961.[14] Sponsored studies stressed the importance of framing our understanding of the church from the perspective of its being missionary by nature.[15] This work has continued through the Commission of World Mission and Evangelism (CWME) within the WCC during the 1980s and 1990s.[16] Evangelicals began to develop this perspective during the 1970s, although it was not until the 1980s that a *Missio Dei* perspective began to reshape the work of many mission organizations.[17] Since the 1970s, the Orthodox Church has incorporated this view into its understanding of the missionary character of the church's liturgical life.[18] Pentecostals have begun to incorporate this way of thinking into their emphasis on the person and work of the Holy Spirit.[19] These developments represent an amazing convergence of thought about mission theology within the diverse streams of the worldwide church.

## Developments in Ecclesiology

While this convergence of thinking was taking place in the discipline of missiology, similar developments were occurring within the discipline of ecclesiology. One of the most significant was the reshaping of the Catholic understanding of the church by Vatican II in the early 1960s. The historic focus of the Roman Church on the institutional character of the church was modified through an emphasis on the church as a community, a people of God.[20] Complementing this in the 1970s, the base community movement in Latin America stressed a holistic view of ministry operating out of a conception of church as a social reality with spiritual empowerment.[21] These views within the Roman Catholic Church have continued to mature with an emphasis on the church as a missional community.

In the past half century, the ecumenical movement has produced excellent biblical and theological work on the missionary nature of the church.[22] Of equal importance has been the renewed emphasis on the visible church's essential unity as being foundational for its witness. Decades-long studies and consultations on both "faith and order" and "life and work" led to the formation of the World Council of Churches in 1948.[23] These studies led the participating church bodies to explore in more detail their historic foundations and their existing institutional and organizational structures. These conversations helped many denominational churches re-examine their ecclesiology and polity. In some cases this resulted in mergers between denominations. In other cases, churches developed a renewed appreciation for their ecclesiological heritage, even as they increasingly recognized the historical, and therefore relative, character of its development.

Another development in the field of ecclesiology in the past several decades parallels that taking place in the field of missiology. Recent studies on the Trinity, especially among Orthodox theologians, have surfaced three different ways of relating a trinitarian understanding of God to our understanding of the church.[24] One focuses on how the essential reality of the church is related to the very being-ness of God. Another focuses on the social reality of the Godhead as the basis for understanding the church as a social community. A third focuses on the specific roles of the three persons of the Godhead in relation to their activity in creation and re-creation. This book draws on all three aspects in understanding the trinitarian foundations for a missiological ecclesiology.

One other source contributing to our thinking about ecclesiology is distinctly North American in origin and consists of a series of applied movements. During the 1960s and 1970s, the church renewal movement placed increased importance on revitalizing existing structures.[25] During the 1970s and 1980s, the church growth movement focused new attention on relating to the social context and planting churches cross-culturally. This movement also attempted, with mixed results due to inadequate theological foundations, to integrate social science methodologies more into the lifeblood of North American churches.[26] The 1980s and 1990s witnessed the emergence of a growing movement of mission-driven, community-based, independent congregations. This has also brought an increased emphasis on achieving effectiveness in established churches and denominational structures.[27] While these movements have not developed thoroughgoing ecclesiologies, they have surfaced important issues and provided insights for the study of ecclesiology.

These insights and contributions from the disciplines of missiology and ecclesiology need to be integrated. We need to relate a view of mission that is based on the redemptive reign of the Triune God in all creation with an understanding of church that views it both as a living community of God's people and as a historical institution. We need to develop a missiological ecclesiology.[28] To do this we must address the interrelationship of the nature, ministry, and organization of the church.

## What a Missiological Ecclesiology Does

Calvin Presbyterian was forty-five years old and had just started a strategic planning process to redefine its future. A planning committee had been formed to lead a yearlong study for developing a comprehensive ministries plan. On this particular evening, the planning committee was to hear a report from the Mission and Evangelism Task Force. Everyone expected to hear an evaluation of the various efforts to recruit new members.

As Carl stood up to report, he felt a little anxious. For two months his task force had wrestled with their mandate. They increasingly had come to realize that mission was not a special activity that a few members were supposed to engage in on behalf of the whole church, but was something that had to invade the whole of the church's life. He began his report by stating this premise, then proceeded to show how mission and evangelism needed to be part of every ministry of the church. Starting with worship and the need to welcome the stranger, he moved to education and the need to plan for incorporating newly received adult converts. He then proceeded through the rest of the church's ministries. He finished by offering the recommendation of his task force that the church's mission and evangelism committee go out of existence and that every committee of the church be mandated with the responsibility to integrate mission into its area of responsibility.

When he finished, there were a few moments of silence before the chairperson spoke up and said, "If we accept your recommendation, the entire church would have to focus on reaching unbelievers."

"Exactly," responded Carl. "That is exactly what we should be doing."

"If we do this," said the chairperson, "most of our members will have to change even how we think about the church."

An ecclesiology expresses our understanding of the church, addressing all aspects of the church's life and ministry. Many ecclesiologies have been based on only a few select biblical images and passages. The selection of images has usually reflected the circumstances facing the church in a particular historical context. Chapter 3 will summarize how this selection process has functioned historically.

In developing a more full-orbed missiological ecclesiology, three aspects of church life must be defined and related to one another: what the church is—its nature; what the church does—its ministry; and how the church is to structure its work—its organization.

The interrelationship of the three aspects is clear. *The church is. The church does what it is. The church organizes what it does.* The nature of the church is based on God's presence through the Spirit. The ministry of the church flows out of the church's nature. The organization of the church is designed to support the ministry of the church. Keeping these three aspects in the right sequence is important when considering the development of a missiological ecclesiology.

## Every Ecclesiology As a Missiological Ecclesiology

To some extent, every historical ecclesiology has functioned as a missiological ecclesiology, even if it has not defined itself as such. There are not multiple missions of God. God is one. His mission in the world is one. The church's understanding of its existence in the world, therefore, regardless of its presence in different contexts, should reflect an understanding of the mission of the Triune God. We can learn much from the study of historical ecclesiologies, even though not all ecclesiologies have either attempted or achieved a holistic perspective on the church's life and ministry. In approaching this task, we must grasp the interrelationship of the nature, ministry, and organization of the church.

## Shaping a Missiological Ecclesiology

What the church believes and confesses about itself shapes its identity and gives direction to its life and ministry. Historically, the church has tended to develop its self-understanding— its ecclesiologies—by affirming certain biblical principles in response to problems within historical settings. While the church must address specific problems that affect its life and ministry, the resulting ecclesiological formulations have also tended to introduce problems into our understanding of the church. Particular ecclesiological formulations were often treated as if they were *the* biblical teaching about the church for all time. Today, we have a variety of ecclesiologies, each of which claims to hold the proper perspective on the church.[29]

Amid these competing views, many today tend to write off this whole discussion as too obscure, academic, or stifling. They usually proceed to make pragmatic decisions about Christian ministry as if the church could be treated primarily in functional or organizational terms.[30] Both of these developments suggest the need to think carefully about how an ecclesiology should be formed.

### The Visible Church

The church, as the term is used in this book, refers to the actual church that exists today in the world in all its multiple forms and structures. There is certainly a sense in which one can speak of an invisible church that consists of all believers throughout the ages. But the biblical record makes it clear that the Spirit is creating a church in the world that is concrete and historical in its existence. It is the nature, ministry, and organization of this visible church that this book addresses.

There are four key sources of information available to us for developing our understanding of the visible church. The relationship of the first three of these is shown in figure 2.

**Figure 2**

**The Visible Church in the World in Relation to Biblical, Historical, and Contextual Realities**

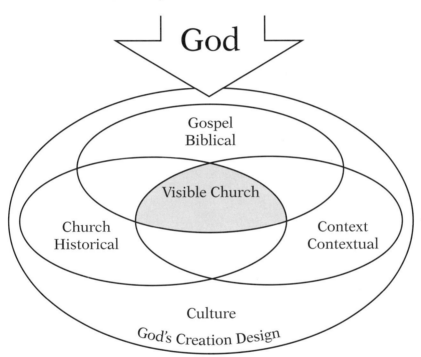

## Biblical Perspectives on the Church

What we believe about the church needs to be based on and consistent with what the Bible teaches. The biblical materials on this subject, however, are both extensive and diverse. Churches in different contexts have drawn on different images and passages and interpreted them from different perspectives in developing their understanding of the church. Ecclesiologies have conceived of the church in such diverse ways as managing the social order, transforming society, confronting society, and living as marginalized communities.[31] The case can be made that biblical narratives and images are available to support all these approaches.

This diversity means that the process of selecting and interpreting biblical materials in developing an ecclesiology requires the church to be aware of the limits of trying to formulate a universal understanding from within a particular context. While the framework of a missiological ecclesiology can be established, its application to different contexts will influence the selection of biblical themes and images. As biblical materials are selectively used, it is important to be explicit about why they are being chosen and how they are being used.

## Historical Perspectives on the Church

The church exists in history as a visible reality, where its existence and life have been shaped by a wide range of cultures. In this regard, all thinking about the church, all ecclesiologies, reflect to some extent the historical circumstances of the eras in which they were developed. In drawing on historical perspectives to shape our ecclesiology, our goal must be to affirm the key insights and teachings of previously formulated ecclesiologies without imposing a previous contextual understanding of the church on our context as if a direct correspondence were possible.

Understanding both the strengths and weaknesses of a variety of historical perspectives can help us in framing a missiological ecclesiology. Every historical ecclesiology addressed in some way the missionary nature of the church, but in many cases did so inadequately. For example, as noted earlier, some ecclesiologies focused primarily on the inner life of the church, while others made mission just one of many tasks the church was to carry out. Still others tied the life and ministry of the church too closely to the state, often subverting the church to national or political ends. While we can learn from these ecclesiologies, we must also test them against the biblical teaching that God is a missionary God to the whole of his creation.

## Contextual Perspectives on the Church

The church never exists in a vacuum. Every ecclesiology, therefore, is developed within a particular cultural context. There is no other way to be the church except within a concrete, historical setting. This means that all ecclesiologies must be seen as functioning relative to their context. This does not mean that they cannot be accurate interpretations of the biblical materials. It does mean, though, that the specifics of any ecclesiology are a translation of the biblical perspective for a particular context. New contexts require new expressions for understanding the church.

We need to develop a missiological ecclesiology that addresses the contextual character of the church. The church is catholic, or universal, in the world. That is, it can exist within any and every culture. The church has the inherent ability to translate the eternal truths of God into relevant cultural forms within any context. In missiology circles this process is referred to as contextualization.[32]

The church, first of all, must explore the teaching of the Bible to understand its own identity, taking care not to compromise biblical truths to cultural patterns. The church, second of all, must seek the guidance of the Spirit to translate these biblical truths so that the redemptive work of God is made relevant to its particular context. As these translations vary with various contexts, the church must also develop structures to maintain community and common confession among all churches.

The three perspectives—biblical, historical, and contextual—provide a helpful framework for thinking about the visible church. But one more perspective is needed to achieve a holistic understanding of the life and ministry of the church. This perspective considers the ongoing work of the Spirit in leading

41

and teaching the church. In figure 3, this fourth perspective is added to the other three.

**Figure 3**

**The Visible Church in the World in Relation
to the Work of the Spirit**

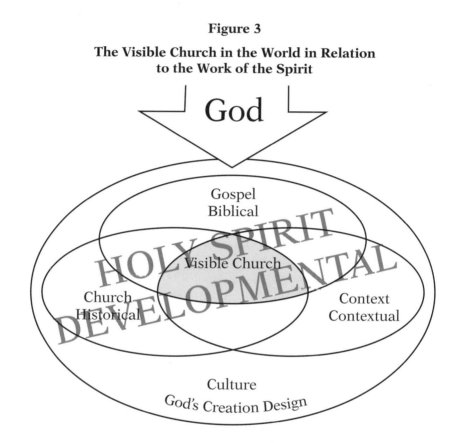

## Developmental Perspectives on the Church

The church is the creation of the Spirit. Every ecclesiology needs to account for the developmental character of the church as the ongoing creation of the Spirit. The church is not static. Ecclesiology is not static. The dynamic person and power of the Spirit are present in the midst of the church. So also, changing contexts require the church to address new issues in understanding its life and ministry. Therefore, as the creation of the Spirit, the church is always developing and changing. We need

A Missional Understanding of the Church

to develop a missiological ecclesiology that takes into account the continued work of the Spirit in leading and teaching the church.

This work of the Spirit is our key resource for shaping the ongoing development of the church. As the church is led and taught by the Spirit, it develops new approaches to ministry and finds new ways to organize its life. Ideally, these new approaches take into consideration biblical teaching and historical learnings about the church while also creatively responding to changing contextual realities. The church can experience this constant renewal only by developing discipline in discerning the leading of the Spirit. Through such discernment, the church becomes the primary means through which God answers its prayer that "thy kingdom come; thy will be done; on earth as it is in heaven" (Matt. 6:10).

## A Missiological Ecclesiology for North America

While a general framework can be developed for understanding a missiological ecclesiology (and this will be done in the following chapters), this framework must always be applied to the church within a specific cultural setting. The continued erosion of the functional "Christendom" developed within the U.S. and Canada, each with its own type of churched culture, is forcing a new discussion of how to be the church in North America.[33] It was always God's intent, even within the mission location of North America, that the church be a missionary church. Some churches have tried to do this, but their approaches have tended to assume a special status for the church in society. Now that the church no longer has a privileged position within North American culture, it is rediscovering its fundamental missionary identity to live as a new community demonstrating God's redemptive reign in the broader society.

The developmental work of the Spirit needs to be affirmed and sought by the church in our changing context. If the church is going to continue to proclaim the Good News to a new gen-

43

eration with integrity, it must do so based on its biblical foundations. If the church is going to provide a new generation with an identity based upon the gospel, it must do so in light of the historical development of the church. If the church is going to share the Word as good news to a new generation with relevance, it must do so in light of changes that continuously reshape the culture. If the church is going to continue to exhibit responsiveness in its life and work, it must do so in light of the Spirit's continued leading and teaching. Understanding the specific context in which the church finds itself is critical for all four tasks.

## Let the Church Be the Church

This book is about understanding the church, about understanding this wonderful and mysterious creation God has planted as his people in the world. It is about understanding the full nature of this creation from a missiological perspective, which is essential if we are to live into the fullness of the redemption God's story invites us to experience. This book is especially about the missionary nature of the church. This nature gives expression to the full character of what the church is to do in fulfilling its ministry and how the church is to organize itself.

It is hoped that those who read this book will discover fresh and exciting ways to reframe some old and wonderful truths about the church. This journey of discovery will not be without pain for any who choose it, for there is much about the church in North America that is in need of careful rethinking. It will require courageous choices in order for necessary changes to be made. Such rethinking and choices for change invite risk and require boldness. But then, that is part of what it means to be the church. Let the church be the church.

A Missional Understanding of the Church

# THREE

# Historical Views of the Church

When John moved to Springdale two years ago, his only experience with church had come during his teens, when he had spent his summers with an aunt who had taken him to a Catholic church. Now in his early thirties, he had not attended any church for years. In the past several months, however, he had joined a noontime Bible discussion group at his office. There he met Michael who befriended him. After a few weeks, Michael invited John to go with him to St. Matthew Lutheran, an ELCA church where Michael was a member.

Not wanting to offend Michael, and being a little curious, John agreed. About halfway into the service, John was wondering what he had gotten himself into. The pastor's robe, the lighting of candles, the altar in the front, the elaborate liturgy sung from a hymnal—all this reminded him of his visits to the Catholic church. He did have to admit, however, that the pastor's message made some sense.

Following the service, Michael asked John what he thought.

"It seemed to be a lot like the Catholic church my aunt used to take me to," John replied. "Is your church related to the Catholic Church?"

"Oh, no!" Michael answered. "Our church broke away from the Catholic Church centuries ago. We believe we are the true church because we engage in the proper ministry of Word and Sacrament."

John didn't reply but did think, "I don't have a clue what you're talking about."

## Ecclesiology

Denominational traditions and beliefs guide the choices and shape the lives of millions of Christians, but often church members know little about how and why they came into existence. Most of these behaviors and beliefs originated within historical ecclesiologies developed through the centuries. They resulted from efforts to apply biblical understandings about the church to specific historical settings. In the process, different churches stressed different issues or came to different conclusions about the same issue.

For many people like John, these historical views don't make much sense. They know that a lot of denominational churches have distinctive practices and beliefs, but they don't know how these relate to a biblical understanding of the church. I believe that understanding something of these historical views can help churches develop a missiological ecclesiology. For many who belong to a distinctive denominational tradition, this chapter will be of interest as it critiques the foundations of their own view of the church, in addition to critiquing those of others. But this critique may not make much sense to readers who have little familiarity with denominational churches; they may prefer to proceed to chapter 4 and read the rest of the book before returning to this chapter.

Ecclesiology helps define the essence of the church—its nature. It gives direction to understanding the work of the church—its ministry. And it identifies the forms and structures that shape the life of the church—its organization.

The Bible itself begins this important discussion, using multiple images and metaphors to explain the church, along with accounts of the church's early ministry and organizational developments. Efforts to interpret and apply these materials within different settings throughout the history of the church have led to the formulation of various ecclesiologies.

## Contextual Ecclesiology

The variety of ecclesiologies that exist result partly from the church's missionary nature. A missionary church seeks to be relevant within a specific cultural setting. In doing so, it develops an understanding of the mission of God in that setting and functions as a type of missiological ecclesiology, even though it may not have developed a thoroughgoing framework for such.

A general biblical framework can be developed for a missiological ecclesiology. However, as various biblical teachings about the church are applied in different contexts, churches will, necessarily, stress different themes. As the church in North America today works to develop a missiological ecclesiology, we must keep in perspective both biblical teaching and insights drawn from the various historical views. The biblical teaching is the subject of chapters 4 through 7. This chapter provides a summary overview of important historical ecclesiologies.

## Historical Ecclesiologies

In the history of the church we encounter a rich and complex story of how the Spirit of God has created, led, and taught the church through the centuries. It is possible, in retrospect, to identify failures in the church and weaknesses in particular ecclesiological perspectives. But we need to take care to appreciate, as well, the struggles of faith of believers in other times and places. There is a tendency in treating the history of ecclesiology to critique earlier views of the church as somehow being deficient in light of later historical developments and learnings.[1] While we need to be aware of the strengths and weaknesses of each ecclesiology, we are best served by first affirming the contributions of each view before critiquing its deficiencies.

The subject of ecclesiology is complex and expansive. A complete critique of it would fill a book in itself. The focus of this chapter is more limited in scope. It reviews briefly five periods in which the church's thinking about itself led to significant developments in defining the church, and it relates these developments to the church in North America. Each period is examined in terms of its historical context; the biblical foundations used;

how the nature, ministry, and organization of the church were addressed; and some of the implications each formulated ecclesiology has had for the subsequent development of the church.

To provide historical perspective, a simplified timeline listing key events in the history of the church is shown (fig. 4).

### Figure 4

### Timeline of Church History and the Development of Ecclesiologies

*the timeline*
*shows his leanings*

|  |  |
|---|---|
|  | 100 Close of New Testament |
|  | 313 Constantine's Edict of Milan |
| 325 Council of Nicea |  |
|  | 380 Christianity as state religion |
| 381 Council of Chalcedon |  |
| Nicene Creed |  |
|  | 800 Charlemagne—Holy Roman Emperor |
|  | 1054 Great Schism—Rome and Orthodox |
|  | 1095–1291 Crusades |
|  | 1350 ff. Renaissance from Italy into Europe |
|  | 1415 John Hus burned at stake |
|  | 1517 Luther posts 95 theses |
| 1530 Augsburg Confession |  |
|  | 1534 Henry VIII forms Church of England |
|  | 1541 Calvin called to Geneva |
|  | 1545 Council of Trent opened |
| 1566 Belgic Confession |  |
|  | 1593 Puritans oppressed in England |
|  | 1607 Settlement at Jamestown |
| 1632 Dordrecht Confession |  |
|  | 1637 Descarte's *Discourse on Method* |
| 1646 Westminister |  |
| Confession | 1648 Peace of Westphalia |
|  | 1687 Newton's *Principia Mathematica* |
| 1689 Locke's *Letter on* |  |
| *Toleration* | 1722 Zinzendorf founds Hernhut |
|  | 1740s Great Awakening in America |
|  | 1776 Revolutionary War in America |
|  | 1781 Kant's *Critique of Pure Reason* |
| 1792 Carey's *Inquiry* |  |
|  | 1800 ff. Modern missions movement |
|  | 1817 Hegel's *Encyclopedia of Philosophy* |
|  | 1820s Second Awakening in America |

48

Historical Views of the Church

# Period 1: The Early Centuries of the Church

Jane was a lifelong member of the American Baptist Church and had been a member of Springdale Baptist since moving into the community twelve years ago. This morning she attended the worship service at Calvin Presbyterian prior to meeting several women from Calvin to discuss the upcoming community Thanksgiving service. The two congregations had shared such a service over the past three years. As the liturgy began, the congregation was asked to stand and recite together the words of the Nicene Creed found in the back of the hymnal.

Not wanting to appear uninformed, Jane joined in, even though the phrase she had learned from her childhood came to mind, "No creed but Christ." When the congregation came to the words, "And I believe one holy catholic and apostolic church," her voice faltered. "My goodness," she thought, "do these people really believe in the Catholic Church?"

Jane's experience is not uncommon for those Christians in North America who are part of churches that do not have a confessional heritage. It is easy for them, like Jane, to confuse the word *catholic* for the Roman Catholic Church instead of understanding it to mean "universal." Corporate reciting of ancient creeds and extensive instruction of young people in certain historical confessions (confirmation or catechism classes) is territory unfamiliar to them. Even many members of churches that have a confessional heritage do not have a strong sense of what these creeds and confessions mean. Yet statements about the church in these creeds and confessions profoundly shape the identity, ministry, and organization of many denominations and their congregations. One such statement occurs in the early creed mentioned above—the Nicene Creed.

In the centuries following the New Testament period, the church encountered opposition and persecution. This resistance was gradually overcome as the Constantinian solution became the order of the day. Movement toward this solution began with the decision by Emperor Constantine to legitimize the church within the empire. By the end of the fourth century, Christianity had become the official religion of the Roman state.

For several centuries as the process of legitimizing Christianity and establishing it as the state church unfolded, a number of general councils were convened. The bishops of the church gathered in these councils to address critical theological issues.

Building on the work of the Council of Nicea in 325, the 150 bishops who convened in 381 as the Council of Constantinople gave final definition to what has become known as the Nicene Creed.[2] In this foundational statement that focused primarily on the christological controversy, the bishops named four attributes of the church with the phrase, "We believe . . . one holy catholic and apostolic Church." These four attributes represented what they believed to be the essential characteristics of the church in the world.

Another early creed, the Apostles' Creed, although it did not come into final form until the eighth century, repeated several of these ideas and added one more in the phrase, "I believe a holy catholic church, the communion of saints."[3] This latter concept identified the social reality of the church as a spiritual community, an idea that has great relevance for today's discussions about the church.

These five attributes came to be the common way of describing the church over the next centuries. This is due largely to the close relationship of these creeds to biblical language and to these early creeds' having gained official acceptance by almost all churches throughout the centuries. The Bible clearly teaches that the church is to be one and holy as it displays the presence of God in the world (see Jesus' prayer in John 17 and the description of the church in 1 Peter 1:15–16; 2:9). The church that was defining this belief about itself existed throughout the known world. This one and holy church was, in fact, also a catholic or universal church. This characteristic was self-evident to the council that formulated this teaching.

Describing the church as apostolic meant that the church was founded on the work of the apostles and prophets. Its inclusion confirmed that the church's authority and teaching were based on the work of the original founders of the church. The

Historical Views of the Church

apostles' authority and teaching were viewed as continuing in the church through the office of the bishop. The image of the church as a communion of saints was also rooted in direct biblical language in the word *koinonia,* which can be translated as "communion" or "fellowship." The church of the fourth century viewed itself as being one, holy, catholic, and apostolic. It was a unified and visible social community that existed in a relational and organizational unity throughout the world, displayed the presence of God, and exercised apostolic authority on his behalf through the office of the bishop.[4]

These early images provide helpful insights into the church's thinking about the nature, ministry, and organization of the church. The nature of the church is most directly addressed in the images of one and holy. Wherever divisions and pollution occur in the church, it is not realizing all that God desires and intends.

The images of catholic, apostolic, and the communion of saints also touched on the nature of the church. Catholic refers to the church as being universal, meaning that it also, by nature, is able to be inherently contextual in any setting. Apostolic refers to the church as representing God's authority on earth. The communion of saints refers to the church's being a social community of Spirit-filled persons.

The ministry of the church is most directly addressed by the image of apostolic, which in its most basic meaning is translated as "one authoritatively sent on a mission." The basic image of the church as apostolic conveys that the church is sent into the world authoritatively by God to participate fully in his redemptive work. In the Nicene Creed's use of this word, however, the primary emphasis was placed on the church's being the authoritative representative of God in the world. That the church was sent into the world was implied, but only in later centuries was the importance of the church's being sent on a mission into the world emphasized more fully.

Other images also implied aspects of ministry. To be one meant that the church should pursue unity. To be holy meant the church should seek to be pure. To be catholic meant the church should seek to be contextually relevant. To be a communion of saints meant the church should function as a Spirit-filled fellowship.

The organization of the church is not addressed directly in any of these images, although some principles are implied. For the church to be one, it must organize itself in ways that promote unity, coordination of purpose, and cooperation of effort. For the church to be holy, it must seek to appropriate the redemptive power of God in its midst. For the church to be catholic, it must organize itself to be flexible and adaptive to new contexts. For the church to be apostolic, it must organize itself to be missional within all its ministry functions and through all its structures. For the church to be a communion of saints, it must promote the building and strengthening of relationships through the exercise of both the fruit and the gifts of the Spirit. While such implications can be drawn out, they were not made fully explicit in the early centuries of the church.[5]

During the vast majority of the medieval period, which ranged from the fifth to the sixteenth centuries, these four attributes represented the functional reality of the church. This thousand years was filled with significant missionary movements, doctrinal developments, and institution building. During much of this time, not only were the attributes affirmed, but they were to a large extent also practiced as commitments of the Roman Catholic Church. However, a significant shift in their usage took place in the late medieval period, the twelfth to the sixteenth centuries. The attributes came increasingly to be viewed as exclusive properties which the Roman Catholic Church alone possessed by virtue of being God's authority on earth.

This approach was initially defined when the Roman Church separated from the Eastern Orthodox Church in 1054. It was further accentuated by a series of pre-Reformation movements within the Roman Church in the fifteenth century that challenged its authority and many of its practices. It became codified as essential when the Counter Reformation fought back in the second half of the sixteenth century against the upstart Protestant Reformers who had dismissed the legitimacy of the Roman Church by identifying it as a false church.[6] In this context, the attributes were often no longer seen as characteristics that were to be consistently demonstrated.

## Period 2: The Protestant Reformation

The speech sounded strange to Jerry. He was in the monthly consistory meeting of the Springdale Reformed Church (RCA) along with the seven other elders who were elected by the congregation to two-year rotating terms. This was his first term as an elder and he often felt there were gaps in his awareness of church structure and procedures. The church had been without a pastor for six months, and the consistory had just received its first report from the search committee.

Detailed selection criteria for calling a new pastor had been defined by the committee in consultation with the consistory, with visionary leadership and organizational skills topping the list. These qualities were being emphasized to help the church reconnect with its changing community. The committee's initial report was not encouraging. They had been able to assemble only a short list of persons who met the criteria, and most of these were not interested in taking a new call.

At this point Bill, an older elder who had served on the consistory many years, made the speech that caught Jerry short. "All the church needs to do is find someone who can faithfully preach the Word and administer the sacraments," Bill said passionately. "We don't need to bother with all this management foolishness."

Jerry, a vice-president in a local high-tech firm wondered, "Where did that come from? What kind of criteria are those for effective leadership? I must be in that 'unfamiliar territory' one more time."

Jerry's experience is not uncommon. As churches today try to identify what kind of leadership is needed for their changing contexts, historical ways of understanding ministry continue to have strong sway. One of the most influential of these was developed at the time of the Protestant Reformation by the Reformers Martin Luther and John Calvin.

53

The Protestant Reformation was the second period of major development in shaping ecclesiology. While the Reformers accepted the Nicene attributes as essential for understanding the church, they tended to place more emphasis on one, holy, and catholic, than on apostolic, for reasons that will be noted below. They sought to identify specific criteria that could be used to test the validity of what constituted a true church, one that legitimately expressed the four attributes. This notion of testing for the true church was developed over against the exclusive claims of authority by the Roman Church, which the Reformers considered to be a false church.

The Reformers had concerns. First, they sought to correct doctrinal error. This was resolved by focusing on the biblical truth of salvation by grace through faith in Christ alone. Second, they sought to shift the locus of authority away from the papacy. This was resolved by locating authority exclusively in the Bible, in contrast to the Roman Church's emphasis on authority residing in the Bible, the tradition of the church, and the office of the papacy. And third, they sought to address perceived abuses in the ministry of the Roman Catholic Church. They did this by identifying distinguishing criteria, or marks, by which the true church could be identified. Such marks first appeared in the Lutheran Augsburg Confession in 1530 as follows:[7] "It is also taught among us that one holy Christian church will be and remain forever. This is the assembly of all believers among whom the Gospel is preached in its purity and the holy sacraments are administered according to the Gospel" (Article VII: The Church).

All the other confessions of the established churches of the Reformation picked up these marks as the distinguishing criteria of the true church. Some branches of the Reformed tradition added a third mark to the list, that of discipline, as can be found in the Belgic Confession, Article 29.[8]

The confessions of this period, in those sections that dealt with the church, usually referenced several of the four attributes identified in the Nicene Creed. This creed was accepted by the Reformers as a legitimate confession of the true church. In addition, the communion of saints of the Apostles' Creed

Historical Views of the Church

was often picked up and given amplification. The attributes most commonly listed were one and holy. On occasion catholic was also included (the Belgic Confession of 1566, Article 27: The Holy Catholic Church. "We believe and confess one single catholic or universal church—a holy congregation and gathering of true Christian believers . . .").

Notably, none of the Reformation confessions referred directly to an apostolic church, although most continued to speak of the apostolic faith and apostolic authority.[9] This was because the Roman Church used the apostolic attribute primarily to legitimize the office of the bishop and the role of the pope based on the authority given to Peter and the other apostles. Partially lost in this deletion was an emphasis on the church's "being authoritatively sent" by God into the world to participate fully in God's mission. The Reformers' downplaying of the apostolic attribute and their shifting of authority from the pope to the Bible were reinforced by their use of the Constantinian solution—the establishment of state churches within their various nations.[10] In place of papal authority, these churches developed confessional standards and church polities to guide the practices of the church. These served as authoritative for maintaining true doctrine and for insuring that the pure preaching of the Word and the proper administration of the sacraments were maintained within the institutional church.

This shift in ecclesiology had profound implications for the church. It was a shift away from the broader categories of the four attributes as essential characteristics of the visible church in the world, to the use of two (or three) marks as criteria for identifying the true church that displayed these four attributes. The intent of the Reformers was to reestablish the mission of God in the world legitimately and authoritatively. Explicit within their approach was the priority given to the institutional character of the church. Attention was focused on the authority of the institutional church for ministering the means of grace through preaching and sacraments. Attention was also focused on insuring that these tasks were carried out properly under the leadership of officially credentialed ordained ministers. Ministry came to be defined primarily in terms of ordained ministers carrying out these responsibilities on behalf of members. The organizational life of the church, which came to be known as church polity, was structured around insuring that these responsibilities were performed decently and in good order.[11]

The use of the marks to test for trueness provided the basis for churches to separate themselves legitimately from that which was false. Affirmation was still given by the first generation of Reformers to the attributes of the church being one, holy, and catholic. However, these attributes increasingly came to be viewed by later generations of Christians as characteristics of the invisible church only. Such an invisible church was conceived as being made up of all believers throughout the ages. This distinction had its roots in the work of theologians in the third through fifth centuries. It was initially conceived by Origen who, under Platonic influence, sought to establish the heavenly church as the ideal for which the earthly (visible) church prepared persons. Augustine made a significant shift in the conception of the invisible church in the fifth century. He used it to establish the distinction between the elect and the nonelect, both of whom might be found in the visible church.[12]

In the Westminster Confession of 1646, the invisible church was confessionally added to the visible church as part of defining the true church. (Chapter XXV. Of The Church. "I. The catholic or universal church, which is invisible, consists of the whole number of the elect, that have been, are, or shall be gathered into one, under Christ. . . . II. The visible church, which is also catholic or universal. . .").[13] This category of the church being invisible was later given primary emphasis among many in the evangelical revival movements of the eighteenth and nineteenth centuries. It was used to maintain a commitment to the church's being one, holy, and catholic, while, in fact, allowing for separation based upon applying some type of criteria for being true and pure. This is significant in that the churches that followed this approach no longer felt compelled to seek the unity of the visible church.

The establishment of the two-marks criteria also tended to shift the church's primary focus from striving to live up to its essential character to the task of maintaining truth. Each church became responsible to determine which churches were true and which were not. While there was concurrence among the early Reformers as to which church was false—the Roman Catholic Church—it didn't take long for the tests of trueness to be applied in a different way. Over the next several centuries, various churches came to use the true-false criteria to test the legitimacy of other Protestant groups, as well as to maintain confessional orthodoxy within their own ranks. This use of these criteria led, and continues to lead, to further divisions within various churches over any number of particular doctrines.[14]

The two marks used to test for the true and pure church introduced significant new ways for thinking about the nature, ministry, and organization of the church. This formulation tended to shift attention from what the church is to what the church does. Although the divine character of the church is inherent within the tasks of the true preaching of the Word and the pure administration of the sacraments, the fuller nature of the church is not as directly addressed as it had been in the earlier four attributes.

What is addressed most directly in the two-marks approach to defining the true church is the ministry of the church. The church is to engage in pure preaching and the proper administration of the sacraments. With this focus on preaching and the sacraments, worship came to be viewed as the primary ministry of the church. In this context, the whole of the ministry of the Word tended to become associated with the preaching event that took place during corporate worship. While other aspects of ministry can be, and sometimes are, related by extension to the function of preaching, what was meant by preaching in the original formulation of the marks was the proclamation of the Word within the regular worship service. While preaching needs to be central to worship, and while worship needs to be central to local church life, the Bible calls the church to engage in other important functions as well, such as fellowshiping, discipling, serving, and witnessing.

The organization of the church was also affected through this formulation of the church. With the focus being on the pure preaching of the Word and proper administration of the sacraments, it became essential to establish who would be officially authorized to carry out these tasks. This led to an emphasis on defining, developing, organizing, and governing an ordained clergy. The church orders, or what have come to be known as church polities, which grew out of the Reformation operate primarily around defining the procedures required for these matters. While some attention was given to the concept of the priesthood of all believers, it usually focused on insuring holiness of life. The notion of a shared gift-shaped ministry of all members was only modestly developed, if at all, under the heavy shadow of an ordained clergy.

Reformation ecclesiology with its testable marks of preaching and sacraments influenced the development of the churches in the years following the Reformation. Established state churches became the norm, while those sects that sought to form free associations based on voluntary choice were persecuted. This established, state-church ecclesiology served as one of the primary contributors to the development of the churches that came to be known as denominations in North America.

## Period 3: The Free Church Movement

Bill and Mary often spent Thursday evenings playing bridge at Joe and Sally's. Bill and Joe worked for the same firm and the couples had become friends. One Thursday, the topic of church came up. Bill and Mary were members of Springdale Southern Baptist, while Joe and Sally were members of St. Mark's Lutheran ELCA.

Joe mentioned that their church had asked the bishop of their synod to get involved in resolving a problem in the congregation. The pastor was evidently involved in some financial indiscretion and needed to be brought under discipline.

Bill commented, "That happened to us one time, but all we had to do was call a congregational meeting and vote the guy out. We believe in the autonomy of the local church."

Different denominations have differing forms of government that call on churches to handle problems in different ways. A major contrast is found between churches with some type of connectional structure that provides for governance over congregations and those systems of self-governing congregations that maintain a connectional association for mutual programming. The latter group came out of the free-church movement.

The free-church movement came into existence during the Protestant Reformation alongside the establishment of state churches. This tradition started with the Radical Reformation or the Anabaptist movement. The primary concerns of the Radical Reformers were to dissociate the church from any official relationship with the state and any oversight from ecclesiastical authorities, and to establish it as a separate community. A good example of this perspective is contained in the Dordrecht Confession (1632) of the Mennonites, which includes the following statement about the church (Article VIII: Of the Church of Christ): "We believe in and confess a visible Church of God, consisting of those, who . . . have truly repented, and rightly believed; who are rightly baptized, united with God in heaven, and incorporated into the communion of saints on earth."[15] This statement placed more direct emphasis on the church as a redeemed social community.

Many Christian groups followed this line of thinking, but during the Reformation period, and for several centuries following, they were usually persecuted by the established churches. This led many of these faith communities to migrate to places of safe haven. A significant number of such communities ended up in North America during and after the seventeenth century. By the eighteenth century, more Christians were adopting and expanding on the principles of church promoted by this movement. The free-church movement includes a broad cross-section of groups with a wide range of theological perspectives. What they share are some basic convictions about the church.

First, these churches are committed to a clear separation of the church's life and ministry from any influence or control by the state. Second, they hold to the necessity of a believer's experiencing a personal conversion and evidencing a personal relationship with God through Christian commitment. And third, they view the church as a visible community made up of such professing believers.

*free Church*

*— free to hire/fire pastor*

These perspectives represent a significant shift away from the Reformers' views, which lodged authority in the institutional church and the means of grace within preaching and sacraments. This shift in perspective has significant implications for ecclesiological thinking about the nature, ministry, and organization of the church.

Regarding the nature of the church, this view connected the personal experience of individual believers in a local fellowship with the reality of the true church of God through all the ages. This tied together the invisible and visible church within the concrete, social character of the congregation. It stressed the importance of all believers maintaining an active Christian commitment. Less developed, however, was the idea of the visible church as a larger reality beyond local congregations or as having any authoritative institutional expression.

Regarding the church's ministry, this view conceived of the church as a body of believers. The church was to be an active fellowship of persons living in relationship with God and one another. This is similar to the perspective of the communion of saints as formulated in earlier centuries. The ministry of the church was to be led by officially appointed leaders, but it was a ministry to be carried out by the body of members. While the ministry of Word and sacraments are important, they are viewed more as means for equipping the saints to be in ministry than as the vehicles of ministry to the saints.

The free-church movement's view of the organization of the church focused on the priority of every believer carrying out responsibilities and having a voice in the congregation. This tradition rapidly gained support during the seventeenth and eighteenth centuries among those influenced by Enlightenment, democratic ideals. Because primary attention was devoted to the visible church as local congregations, little attention was given to the broader organization of the church through official offices and larger organizational structures.

Although this movement was usually marginalized in the European context, many of the themes of the ecclesiology of this movement became influential in those denominations that were given birth in the emerging nations of the U.S. and Canada during the eighteenth and nineteenth centuries. This ecclesiology continues to serve as a primary influence in shaping the development of the church in North America today.

# Period 4: Pietism, Mission Societies, and the Modern Missions Movement

Henry was amazed as he sat through the pastor's new member orientation. Henry and his family were joining the Lighthouse Christian Missionary Alliance (CMA) church in Springdale. This church was very outreach-oriented and Henry had come to a personal faith in Christ through a home Bible study conducted by one of the members. After growing up as a Methodist, Henry had become inactive as an adult.

The pastor was explaining the history of the CMA, noting that the denomination actually started as a mission society before being organized as a denomination. It still thought of itself in missionary terms. This sounded a little strange to Henry, but he could see how the whole church seemed to be organized around reaching others in the community.

The relationship between church and mission has a complex history which became more complicated with the emergence of the modern missions movement. During this time, scores of mission societies in Europe and parachurch structures in North America were formed, usually outside of the institutional church. The theology that usually guided their work was rooted in an evangelical movement known as pietism.

Throughout church history there have always been movements that expressed a more organic understanding of the church. Examples include many of the monastic movements of the medieval period and pre-Reformation movements such as the Brethren of Common Life, Waldensians, and the followers of Wycliffe and Hus. Most never formulated any official ecclesiology. Following the Reformation, a similar movement developed within some of the state churches of Europe. By the late seventeenth and early eighteenth centuries, many of these state churches were stymied by traditionalism and a rationalistic con-

61

fessionalism. The movement that grew up in reaction to this was pietism, especially within the Lutheran Church of Germany. Franke and Spener were key leaders of the movement, but it was Count Zinzendorf, a former student of theirs, who developed some ecclesiological thinking in light of pietism.[16]

Zinzendorf's conception of the church went beyond the pietist view of a "church within the church." Each denomination was conceived to be a school of wisdom within which there were true believers. The Moravian Brethren were seen as an ecumenical apostolate that was to work among these various traditions to achieve a worldwide fellowship.[17] Zinzendorf's true believers were those who shared a personal experience of faith, a passion for personal piety, and a zeal to share their faith with others. This personalized piety became a great force for missions activity under Zinzendorf's influence, especially when it was married to the organizational structure of the Moravian community. Other groups picked up on this personalized piety and missions focus as central for expressing the organic character of the church. Of special importance in this regard was John Wesley who gave birth to the Methodist movement in England after being influenced by the Moravians.

The concept of a specialized group of persons engaging in missions was further developed in the work of William Carey at the end of the eighteenth century. He worked within a Calvinist Baptist tradition that held to a strict view of God's election and predestination. This tradition understood the Great Commission of Matthew 28 to have been fulfilled by the first-century apostles. Carey reacted to these views and wrote an important treatise titled *An Enquiry into the Obligations of Christians to Use Means for the Conversion of the Heathens*. In this document, Carey added two critical concepts to ecclesiological thinking. One was the obligation to obey the Great Commission as a primary responsibility of the church. This led to missions becoming more focused as one of the necessary tasks of the church. The other was the forming of a special association of committed believers as the primary vehicle for conducting and supporting this work, which became the mission society. Carey's own words are interesting to read on this point:[18]

62

Suppose a company of serious Christians, ministers, and private persons, were to form themselves into a society, and make a number of rules respecting the regulation of the plan, and the persons who are to be employed as missionaries, the means of defraying the expense, etc. This society must consist of persons whose hearts are in the work, men of serious religion and possessing a spirit of perseverance; there must be a determination not to admit any person who is not of this description, or to retain him longer than he answers to it.

Pietism, Great Commission theology, and mission societies have had a profound influence in shaping understandings of the nature, ministry, and organization of the church.

Pietism had a great impact on how the nature of the church was seen. In this view, the focus shifted to the individual believer. One's personal experience with God became the center of God's redemptive work in the world. This tended to displace the church to secondary status, whether in its institutional form or in its existence as a social community.

The focus of the ministry of the church was redirected in two ways. First, in pietistic views, ministry was primarily directed toward cultivating means to achieve personal discipleship. Second, in mission-society views, missions was added as a necessary act of obedience for the church, an act which was to be carried out by a few specialized persons.

The organization of the church was also affected by these views. Pietism displaced the importance of ordained clergy as necessary to minister the means of grace. This significantly undermined the efforts of the established churches in Europe to maintain authority. It also undermined the efforts of emerging denominations in North America to claim any right of church authority over Christians beyond their own members. The mission society movement led to the formation of scores of alternative missions structures in the church.[19] These newly created missional structures became the primary organizational form through which European churches engaged in missions over the next century. Their North American equivalents became the parachurch and faith-mission structures, along with denominational boards and agencies.[20]

Both the pietistic movement and the formation of mission societies were foundational for stimulating and channeling Protestant missionary efforts. Visionary leaders like Zinzendorf and Carey developed strategies to engage in missions toward peoples of various cultures and religions in other lands, of which they now were becoming aware. Their strategies both reflected and reacted to the existing ecclesiologies of their day. Zinzendorf, for example, sent Moravian missionaries out under the sponsorship of the Danish crown.[21] This reflected the ecclesiology of established state churches conducting official missions activities through the mission society structure, but only within their own domains or colonies. The work of these early pioneers became the foundation of what we now think of as the modern missions movement that spanned the period of the late 1700s to the mid-1900s.

This movement has profoundly impacted the development of ecclesiology.

First, the ecclesiology transferred to the mission field was either the task-oriented, mission-society model, or the transplanted ecclesiologies of state churches and voluntaristic denominations. There was a lack of attention to context, a lack of awareness of the need to translate these principles within non-Western settings. This provoked significant reactions by these emerging churches in later decades. The ecclesiological developments growing out of these reactions make up a later part of the story.

Second, the proliferation of structures carrying out missions as task, both within and beyond the institutional churches, has greatly complicated the process of developing a coherent view of the church in North America. Each organization develops its own identity, rationale, and resource base. A missiological ecclesiology for North America needs to address how the church is to understand itself in the midst of this proliferation of organizations.

Third, the concept of missions became that of a specialized task carried out by the church through conducting evangelism at home and sending missionaries abroad; or the specialized task of separate organizations that had little or no relationship with the institutional church. Lost was the conception of the church as apostolic, as being missionary by its very nature. This confusion between mission and missions, as discussed in chapter 2, continues to plague the church today.

Fourth, many of the organizations developed during the modern missions movement were shaped by strong leaders who had strong charisma and could articulate a focused vision. Such organic expressions of the church continue to be developed today in a variety of ways including parachurch organizations, faith missions, interdenominational movements, and single-purpose causes. Within these organizations, the focus is usually on applied faith and practical biblical truths rather than on theological systems or formulated confessions. Each legitimates its ministry as fulfilling some biblical function, usually one the established churches have insufficiently addressed. But few ever work out an explicit ecclesiology. In fact, many of these movements and organizations see ecclesiology as a hindrance to their work because the formal structures of the institutional church, associated as they are with explicit ecclesiologies, are often viewed as part of the problem they seek to overcome.

# Period 5A: The Denominational, Organizational Church

Fellowship Community was started in the Springdale community in the late 1970s. It originally adapted a "ministry center" style that sought to eliminate the cultural barriers associated with so many of the denominational churches. Fellowship Community attracted scores of young families who were turned off by other churches. By the late 1980s, the church shifted toward a more seeker-sensitive approach that made personal witness a more explicit expectation of membership.

Quite a few of the earlier members began to drift over to Faith Community, which was started in the 1990s. Faith's basic format was a Bible-teaching pulpit ministry along with intentional small groups. Pastor Bob from Fellowship Community was on the phone with a family that had recently made this move. He was struck by their comment that, "After all, the church is a voluntary organization. If it's no longer meeting our needs, why shouldn't we move on to some place that can?"

The church as a voluntary organization meeting personal needs—where did we ever get this view of the church? During the eighteenth century, a fundamentally new way of thinking about the church emerged in the form of the denominational, organizational church. This development took place mostly within the American colonies in an effort to legitimize the variety of Christian traditions immigrating into the same area.

The idea of the denominational, organizational church had even earlier roots in the free-church movement, especially in England. In the aftermath of the Anglican persecution of the Puritans, and in response to the growing ascendancy of the Scottish Presbyterians, the English Independents developed a theological rationale to give legitimacy to free churches.[22] Basic to this rationale were the effort to rediscover the essential aspects of the New Testament church and the belief that the visible unity of the church needed to transcend theological and organizational differences. The term used for this new form of church was "denomination."[23]

The theological rationale developed in England found ready acceptance in the American colonies, where diverse traditions and organizational forms commingled dynamically. In this context, the concept of "denomination" continued to develop. As Martin Marty points out:

> The first half-century of national life saw the development of evangelicalism. . . . within (this) empire, ministers and lay leaders served as the custodians of faith and values. They busied themselves gathering followers, organizing them into effective units, ministering to their needs, judging their ways of life, and exhorting them to take their place in the world. For such activities it was necessary to invent new forms or radically rework old ones. The result was a network of denominations, local churches, educational institutions, revivals, and agencies. . . . it is true that nothing so basic as this change had occurred in the administrative side of Christian church life in fourteen hundred years. . . .[24]

This new way of thinking about the church theologically and organizationally was reinforced by another eighteenth-century influence—the Enlightenment with its social-contract theory. Social theorists wanted to establish a foundation for society beyond tradition, the divine right of kings, and the domain of the church. As an alternative, they considered an individual's natural rights and rational abilities to be the starting points for constructing a social contract. In this view, freely associating individuals come together in rational agreement based on shared principles as the basis of forming a new society. John Locke, one of the most articulate of these thinkers, wished to separate the social order from the rule of the king and the control of the church. His view of the voluntary character of society spilled over into his conception of the church:

> I take (it) to be a voluntary society of men joining themselves of their own accord in a church order to the public worshipping of God in such manner as they judge acceptable to Him. . . . I say it is a free and voluntary society. Nobody is born a member of the church. . . . since the joining together of several members into this church-society . . . is absolutely free and spontaneous, it necessarily follows that the right of making its laws can belong to none but the society itself; or at least to those whom the society by common consent has authorized thereunto.[25]

This view of the church as an organization formed by the voluntary association of self-selecting individuals quickly gained wide acceptance. Understanding its influence is foundational for sorting out present-day ecclesiologies in North America.

The modern conception of the church as being essentially denominational, organizational, and voluntaristic has profound implications for our understanding of the nature, ministry, and organization of the church. In this view, while the divine aspects of the nature of the church may be included confessionally, the church's identity is shaped primarily by its social organization. Because of the voluntary, individualistic nature of joining this social organization, its focus tends to be on the rights and privileges associated with membership, not on a covenantal commitment to the community and its values.

In terms of the church's ministry, this view tends to focus attention on methodological strategies meeting the needs of the individual members. Implicit in this view is that unless individual members are satisfied, they are free to change their voluntary association.

The church's organization is also impacted by this view. Because the church is seen primarily as a social organization, endless attention is invested in developing, redeveloping, and adjusting the form of the organization to achieve ministry effectiveness.

The denominational, organizational church functions as a voluntary association of congregations that are committed to a common confession, polity, and/or Christian tradition. The rise of the denomination was for the most part a pragmatic solution to a new situation. Multiple congregations of different traditions found themselves occupying the same territory without any one of them having dominion. After the Revolutionary War in America when the states united into a national government, there was a parallel development in the formation of national, denominational organizations with regular assemblies and structured boards.[26] The rapid proliferation of this new form of church among Protestants helped to shift the focus away from a true church versus false church testing. The new situation ushered in a type of friendly competition as the various denominations took responsibility for churching the new nation.

Similar developments took place in Canada. This began with the displacement of some denominational groups from the American colonies to Canada following the Revolutionary War. These groups began to challenge the dominance of the Anglican Church that was established in all of the provinces except Quebec, where the Roman Catholic Church was established. In the first half of the nineteenth century, the immigration of various ethnic churches into Canada furthered denominational development. After confederation in 1867, the pattern of churches forming national denominational structures with accompanying boards and agencies became the norm.[27]

The emergence of the denominational, organizational form of the church, with its voluntary-association congregations, functioned as an overlay on top of existing ecclesiological thinking. Most denominations simply accepted the reality of the denominational form and worked more at developing their internal ecclesiology and polity than at justifying their existence. Some attention was given to biblical foundations, but for the most part these denominations, both those transplanted from European state-churches and those born in North America, used Reformation ecclesiology to shape their church identities and practices. The primary focus was on the ministry of Word and sacraments, accompanied by concerns for ordination, ministerial authority, and procedures for placing and governing pastoral leadership.

Some denominations achieved a unique marriage of European traditions and North American democracy, such as the Methodists who merged the historic role of bishops with democratized procedures in local congregations. Other denominations created entirely new structures out of the democratic tradition such as the Christian Church (Disciples of Christ). In every denomination, the social-contract theory of voluntary associations became deeply imbedded in North American ecclesiology. This has produced an ecclesiology with a strong bias toward treating the church primarily as an organization.

## Period 5B: Denominations As Marginalized Minorities

Calvary African Methodist Episcopal Zion had a rich heritage. It began in the late 1800s as one of the first African-American congregations in the city and was deeply involved in the Civil Rights movement of the 1960s. A strong tradition of leadership in the African-American community characterized its ministry, largely because a significant number of its members were college educated and fairly well-to-do. This now presented a problem.

A decision was made in 1985 to relocate the church to the Springdale community since so many of the members were buying homes in this suburb. It had been a real fight, with nearly one-third of the congregation choosing to stay in the old neighborhood and continue as a church in that location. Pastor Wilson had recently accepted a call to Calvary and was struggling to find the right theme to deliver to the members of his congregation. Should he affirm their new affluence and growing influence in the community, or should he call them to continue to be advocates for the disadvantaged?

Denominationalism has displayed a capacity for helping groups that are marginalized in society to establish a communal identity. Ethnic-based denominations are deeply woven into the denominational story. Many of them, transplanted to North America through immigration, brought ecclesiological heritages out of which they soon formed ethnic denominations. Many of these denominations were forced to maintain their ethnic isolation, and used their adapted ecclesiologies as frameworks for providing ministry primarily to their own members and children.

Among one marginalized North American population, however, a denominational story has unfolded that goes beyond the formation of ethnic identity. During the nineteenth century in the United States, as more of the oppressed black population began to accept Christianity, the church came to play a critical role in shaping a corporate identity and social cohesion for this people.

Some black, denominational churches had been formed in the late 1700s and early 1800s by the freemen, but the vast majority of blacks were slaves. Initially, some white churches allowed blacks to participate in their worship services in restricted ways through segregated seating in the balconies. But as slavery became more entrenched, most blacks were forced to develop their church life in other ways. During this period, the "invisible church" developed within the black community. After the Civil War, much of this invisible church merged into the existing black denominations, although some new organizations were also formed.[28]

This type of denomination functioned quite differently from that developed by the white, European immigrants. Since it was the one institution over which blacks were allowed to have

Historical Views of the Church

control, it had a much more holistic ecclesiology. The reflections of E. Franklin Frazier on these points are helpful:

> . . . it was not what remained of African culture or African religious experience but the Christian religion that provided the new basis of social cohesion. . . . One must study the influence of Christianity in creating solidarity among a people who lacked social cohesion and a structured social life.
> . . . when the Negro became free . . . an organized religious life became the chief means by which a structured or organized social life came into existence among the Negro masses.[29]

The church in the black community functioned out of a different ecclesiology than that found in the white community. The black churches worked only indirectly out of European ecclesiological foundations as they emulated white forms. But they drew deeply from biblical thinking about the church as a social community that was holy, and that was to be holistic in shaping every aspect of life. This indigenous ecclesiology was profoundly biblical in many ways, but developed for the most part without the benefit of much theological or historical reflection. It was born out of the practical need for a functional ecclesiology that helped the black population survive severely oppressive conditions.

The essential principles of this ecclesiology, as with many others, were defined after the fact. This is how contextual ecclesiological development normally happens. What insights does the African-American church give us on the nature, ministry, and organization of the church?

The black church was both a community of God's people and a human social organization. The black experience of suffering fostered the need for a shared space where the harshness of the world could be set aside and hopes could be nurtured. The black church provided space for both. This was not escapism, for the approach to ministry developed by the black church was to view all of life as the direct responsibility of the church. The black church blended into one ministry care for its own well-being and responsibility for the broader community.

71

The black church functioned in many ways as a parallel community within the broader white society. It was a social organization of the people of God living as a nation within the nation. It was responsible for shaping the whole of black life. Organizationally, the black church tended to follow patterns established by the white denominations. The same set of denominational, organizational arrangements, which reflect both European traditions and American pragmatism, can be found among both white and black denominations as can the problems associated with these structures.

Many of the principles embodied in the black church are useful for developing a missiological ecclesiology for the North American church. While the black church experience is singled out here, the ecclesiology shaped through the experience of other marginalized groups in the North American story can be similarly instructive.

## Ecclesiology in the Twentieth Century

The twentieth century, in many ways, has been a century focused on the doctrine of the church, as chapter 2 illustrated. The developments of recent decades have done much to reshape and refine our understanding of historical ecclesiologies. These developments have also moved the church in some new directions in considering more fully its participation in the mission of God in the world. All these developments are leading the church into a clearer understanding of a missiological ecclesiology.

# The Church and the Redemptive Reign of God

Sam, raking leaves in his backyard, stopped to look around at his neighbors who were doing the same thing. Two houses down was Aaron, an African-American who worked for one of the high-tech firms near Springdale. He and his family had moved into the neighborhood two years ago and were members of Calvary AME Zion. Sam caught Aaron's eye and waved. "He seems friendly enough," thought Sam, "but do I really want to get to know him?"

Sam did not think of himself as a racist, but he had to admit that he had thought from time to time about relocating as the African-American and Hispanic groups continued to move into the community. It wasn't that he was concerned about property values. In fact, property values were rising. But the cultures of these two groups just seemed so different from his own white heritage.

His thoughts drifted to last week's sermon at his church, Calvin Presbyterian. The pastor had noted how the kingdom reign of Christ brings a new order into our human relationships. In the church on earth, heaven has already begun. Christians living into Christ's redemptive reign live by eternal values in their earthly choices. "We both claim to be Christians," Sam thought. I wonder what heaven on earth is supposed to look like for Christians of different races living in the same neighborhood?"

# The Kingdom of God

The concept of the kingdom of God has been defined variously as Christ's rule in the hearts of people; the presence of the institutional church; a thousand-year reign of Christ yet to be fulfilled; the providential care of God to sustain his creation; and the ideal moral life modeled in the example of Jesus.[1] These various interpretations are rooted in different theological assumptions, and they have profound implications for how the church and its members relate to the world.

The diversity of these interpretations illustrates something of the complexity we encounter in trying to sort out the meaning of the kingdom of God. Sam's earthly choices reflecting eternal values would be quite different depending on which interpretation he gave to the kingdom of God. Coming to clarity on the meaning of the kingdom of God is foundational to understanding the mission of God in the world.

## The Kingdom As God's Redemptive Reign

The field of biblical studies over the past half century has seen an emerging consensus that an understanding of the church must start with an understanding of the kingdom of God.[2] More specifically, it must start with the announcement of the inauguration of God's redemptive reign in the person and presence of Jesus.[3] The redemptive reign of God must serve as the foundation for defining the nature, ministry, and organization of the church. The church must find its core identity in relation to God's redemptive reign as introduced by Jesus in his announcement that the "kingdom of God has come near" (Mark 1:14–15).

This perspective is shared today by Christians from a wide range of church traditions. It has become a common point of reference in mission theology and in much of the writing taking place in the field of ecclesiology. But it has not yet worked its way into the life of many of the denominations, missional structures, and local congregations that make up the North American church. Most of these still assume that the church is to be understood primarily either in institutional, functional, or organizational terms. There is a lack of emphasis on God's redemptive reign shaping the church as a social community. In understanding the Spirit's creation of the church, it is crucial to begin with an understanding of the kingdom of God as introduced in the ministry of Jesus.

Jesus established the meaning of the kingdom of God as God's redemptive reign. The word translated "kingdom" in the New Testament, *basileia*, refers primarily to the right of a king to reign. The idea of kingdom as territory or location is secondary, and when Jesus uses the term this way, it refers to the whole of creation.[4] The basic idea of the kingdom is that God in Jesus powerfully entered human history with a reign that reestablished life on the basis of redemptive power. This reign of God looks toward the sovereign rule of God as creator and sustainer of all of life—God's providence. But this reign of God is about the dynamic presence of God's redemptive power confronting the forces of evil and restoring life to its fullness— God's redemptive work. This fullness of life looks back to the intent of creation design and forward to the promises associated with the new heavens and new earth. This redemptive reign has two dimensions: it is already present, but also future in some aspects.

Understanding the kingdom of God as God's dynamic, redemptive reign has profound implications for our understanding of the nature of the church. The relationship of the concepts of the kingdom of God and the church is at the heart of unraveling many of the problems associated with church life today.[5] It is also central to a proper understanding of a missiological ecclesiology.

This chapter first presents an overview of the redemptive reign of God as announced by Jesus. This is followed by a fuller treatment of the meaning of God's redemptive reign as revealed through God's creation purposes and his redemptive plan throughout the ages. The third section brings these two themes together to shed light on the missionary nature of the church and the church's role in God's mission in the world.

The Church and the Redemptive Reign of God

# Jesus Announces the Reign of God

The message presented in the four Gospels is clear: Jesus is introducing a new reality into human history. While this intervention is dynamically connected to God's redemptive work presented throughout the Old Testament, new ground is being broken. This new reality will reshape the course of human events. No longer will humanity be divided between Jews and Gentiles. There will be a new dividing line that fulfills a key Old Testament expectation, a division between the children of God and the children of the evil one (see Gen. 3:15 and the seed of the woman and the seed of the serpent). Jesus' presence in the world as the incarnate Son of God is central to the inauguration of this new reality. Jesus draws on the "Son of Man" image from Daniel 7 to define his identity for carrying out this work.[6] This is a clear claim that he is divine and that he is the fulfillment of Old Testament expectations for the coming of the Messiah-King.

Jesus makes his death and resurrection central to inaugurating the redemptive reign of God. The cross event is the watershed of human history. In this decisive moment the forces of evil are defeated and the full power of the redemptive reign of God through the Spirit invades human space. In this invasion, Jesus anticipates the creation of a new type of community, a community created by the Spirit.

Jesus draws on another Old Testament image in presenting the necessity of his death and resurrection, the image of the "suffering servant," best summarized in Isaiah 53.[7] The divine king of Daniel will usher in God's redemptive reign in human history as a suffering servant. This style of ministry is also to mark the community to be created by the Spirit.

Those around Jesus had trouble understanding that the divine king of Daniel 7 would accomplish the salvation work of the suffering servant of Isaiah 53. Some were looking for a national king to overthrow the Roman oppression. Others, such as John the Baptist, were looking forward to the eschatological fulfillment of the end of time. Both perspectives can be found among Jesus' followers. Jesus' teaching about the redemptive reign of

The Church and the Redemptive Reign of God

God in the midst of this confusion is instructive for us to understand both his person and his ministry.

## John the Baptist's Announcement of the Kingdom

John the Baptist preached a repentance for the forgiveness of sins in the context of announcing that the "kingdom of heaven has come near" (Matt. 3:2). His call to repentance was strong and clear and presented with conviction. He associated with the coming of the kingdom a great "wrath to come" (3:7). The contrast he drew between his baptism and the baptism of the one he was introducing highlights this point.

John's baptism was with water, but the one coming after him would baptize with "the Holy Spirit and fire" (3:11). John's expectation was in line with the Old Testament prophets who had foretold the Day of the Lord, the time when human history would end, when God would establish the believing community of Israel, and when God would judge the nations for their disobedience.[8] In this light John was calling for a repentance of sin and offering a baptism that symbolized this repentance.

**Figure 5**

**John's View of the Coming of the Kingdom**

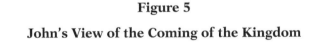

Day of the Lord

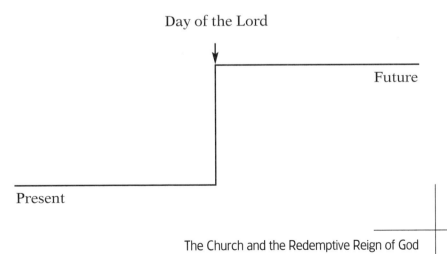

Future

Present

John was an Old Testament prophet, the last of this line (Matthew 11). As an Old Testament prophet, John viewed the coming Day of the Lord as the decisive moment of human history when God's eschatological blessing on the redeemed would begin (the baptism of the Holy Spirit), and his judgment of evil would be completed (baptism with fire) (see fig. 5).

In time, John came to wonder if something was wrong. While it was not fully clear whether the blessing of the Holy Spirit had begun, it was clear that the baptism of fire on the evildoers had not taken place. What had happened? Was Jesus really the Messiah?

## Jesus' Announcement of God's Redemptive Reign

After being baptized by John, Jesus began to develop his own following, and many of his early disciples came to him from John's ministry. Others were attracted to Jesus' message. During his first year of ministry, he related to these followers with little public attention. But at a decisive moment—the imprisonment of John the Baptist—he took his message public. Matthew, Mark, and Luke all record this turning point, but Mark is explicit in associating it with Jesus' announcement regarding the reign of God. "The time is fulfilled, and the Kingdom of God has come near"(Mark 1:14).

This turning point in Jesus' ministry was followed by two years of proclaiming the message about God's redemptive reign. During these two years he also trained his close followers, preparing them for his death. Isaiah 53 had to be fulfilled. The only question was whether the people of Israel would welcome Jesus as their king who had to suffer and die, or whether they would participate in putting him to death by rejecting his offer of salvation.

Jesus' announcement that God's redemptive reign was present in his person and message was similar to John's announcement, but Jesus understood it differently. This became obvious when John the Baptist, now in prison, sent several of his disciples to Jesus with the question, "Are you the one who is to come, or are we to wait for another?" (Matt. 11:2). Jesus' answer was indirect, but to the point. He told these followers of John to go and tell John what they "hear and see" (11:4).

In summarizing what his followers were hearing and seeing, Jesus used phrases that referenced the great Old Testament prophecy from Isaiah 61 about the "year of the Lord." Jesus' point was self-evident. All of the great redemptive aspects of the anticipated kingdom of God were present in Jesus' ministry: the blind saw, the lame walked, lepers were cleansed, the deaf heard, the dead were raised, and the Good News was being proclaimed to the poor. All the anticipated blessings of the presence of the Holy Spirit were already present. The baptism of the Holy Spirit had begun. But what about the judgment of evil?

It was this point that confused John the Baptist. While the work of the Holy Spirit was evident, the judgment of evil was being delayed. This could not be the Day of the Lord as John understood it.

**Figure 6**

**Jesus' Presentation of the Redemptive Reign of God**

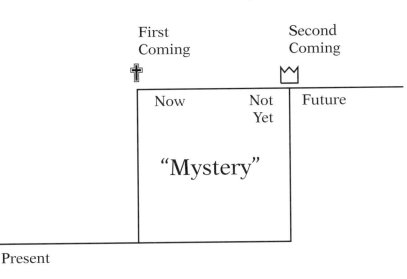

The Church and the Redemptive Reign of God

Jesus made clear that these two aspects of God's reign, the baptism of the Holy Spirit and the baptism by fire, were in fact separate events, separated by the period of time between his first coming as the incarnate Son of Man and suffering servant, and his second coming as the reigning Son of God and conquering king (see fig. 6).

Jesus' followers struggled to understand this reality. How could the future have already begun? How could it be that certain features of the kingdom were delayed? What was this redemptive reign of God all about?

## The Mystery of the Kingdom

On the one hand, the kingdom of God is already present. God's redemptive power has fully entered into history through the Spirit and is now at work in the world. On the other hand, the final judgment of sin and evil has been delayed. The kingdom of God is both present and delayed. It is both "already" and "not yet." This is what Jesus referred to as the mystery of the kingdom (see especially Matthew 13, Mark 4, and Luke 8, 13).

The disciples had trouble understanding this. So Jesus told them a series of parables to clarify these two aspects of the reign of God, and he performed numerous miracles to illustrate the power associated with this reign.

### Parable of Wheat and Weeds

One of the most penetrating parables for understanding the already–not-yet character of God's reign is the parable of the wheat and weeds (Matt. 13:24–30, 36–43). A master sows wheat in a field, but the enemy comes by night and sows weeds. As the wheat and weeds grow together, the servants ask the master whether they should pull up the weeds. The master says that they must grow together, for pulling up the weeds would also pull up the wheat. Their roots are intertwined.

Jesus' explanation of the parable is to the point. "The one who sows the good seed is the Son of Man; the field is the world,

80

and the good seed are the children of the kingdom; the weeds are the children of the evil one, and the enemy who sowed them is the devil; the harvest is the end of the age, and reapers are angels. Just as the weeds are collected and burned up with fire, so will it be at the end of the age" (13:37–40). The good seed is present in the world. The Holy Spirit is already at work forming the children of the kingdom of God. But the baptism of fire has been delayed. It will come in a final judgment at a time of God's choosing. God's reign is both already and not yet.

Jesus clearly expects there to be a new dividing line between the children of the kingdom—the anticipated church—and the children of the evil one. He also expects the children of the kingdom to have the insight, power, and perspective to live as a redeemed community in a fallen and broken world. They will fully participate in every aspect of life but will do so on the basis of a different set of values, values shaped by the redemptive reign of God and made effective by the power of the Spirit.

## Forgiving Sins and Healing the Paralyzed Man

Jesus demonstrated an important truth about God's reign in his encounter with the paralyzed man (see Mark 2:1–12). Because Jesus was surrounded by the crowds, four friends let the man down through the roof in front of Jesus. Impressed with the faith of the friends, Jesus told this man, "Son, your sins are forgiven" (5). It is clear that the friends expected Jesus to heal the paralyzed man. They probably were not prepared for what they heard. But it was the scribes who caught the focus of Jesus' forgiving the man's sins. They whispered, "Blasphemy! Who can forgive sins but God alone?" (7). This, of course, was Jesus' point. He was God, and so had authority to forgive sins.

To demonstrate this authority, Jesus asked whether it was easier to say the man's sins were forgiven or to tell him to walk. His point was clear. The kingdom of God is about the forgiveness of sins. It is about reconciling sinful people to a holy God. The great drama of redemption was now unfolding before their eyes as Jesus announced the good news of the kingdom. But he didn't stop there. He also proceeded to heal the man physically, "so that you may know that the Son of Man has authority on earth to forgive sins" (10).

The redemptive reign of God is about the power of God at work forgiving sins. This is central. But it is also about the children of the kingdom experiencing the power of the redeemed life within the "already" of God's reign. The healing speaks to the possibilities of this redeemed living. It is God's power that is to shape a new community of people who will follow him. The fuller realities of this power are revealed in several other experiences in Jesus' ministry.

## Resisting the Temptations of Satan

In Jesus' wilderness temptations (Matt. 4:1–11), we catch a glimpse of the cosmic battle being waged with the inauguration of God's reign. The three temptations concern food, what sustains life; safety, what controls life; and glory, who governs life. On all three points, Jesus makes it clear that the kingdom of God operates by a different set of values than the kingdoms of this world.

In reference to what sustains life, Jesus makes it clear that the deeper reality of human existence finds its satisfaction and fulfillment in knowing God. This knowledge comes through God's Word. In reference to what controls life, Jesus makes it clear that God is in charge of the circumstances of life. Trusting in God provides true security for those who follow God. In reference to who governs life, Jesus makes it clear that everything belongs to God and that worshiping God alone is the focal point of being the true children of the kingdom.

These temptations and his defeating them represent the framework of the power encounter that is at work in human history. The children of the kingdom also live by a different set of values. They are guided by a different set of expectations. And they live out of a different source of power. This event confirms the character of the kingdom of God. Those who would follow Jesus must realize they are entering into a cosmic conflict with the enemy, a conflict they can win only by the power of the Spirit.

The Church and the Redemptive Reign of God

## Binding the Strong Man

Jesus spells out the nature of this victory in his teaching about binding the strong man (Luke 11:14–23). The occasion for this teaching is his casting out a demon and the accusation by some that he did so by the power of Beelzebul, the ruler of demons. Jesus points out the faulty logic of the accusation by reminding them that a house divided against itself cannot stand. How can Satan be divided against himself? To drive the point home even further, Jesus inquires of his accusers by whom their own exorcists cast out demons.

Jesus then teaches two important truths. He first notes that if it is by the "finger of God that I cast out the demons, then the kingdom of God has come to you" (20). The kingdom of God is not just about ideas and words; it is also about power and confrontation. The children of the kingdom should expect to be involved in a power encounter with the evil one, a conflict between kingdoms that requires reliance on God's power for victory.

The second point Jesus teaches on this occasion is that God's redemptive reign as inaugurated in the person and presence of Jesus has defeated and bound the strong man, Satan. The children of the kingdom are now to participate in this great redemptive drama by plundering the strong man's stronghold. They are to reclaim lost territory by bringing back to right relationship with God what was lost in the fall. The enemy has been defeated and is bound. Although his power still operates, he has encountered someone stronger. Greater is he who is in the children of the kingdom than he who is in the world.

The redemptive reign of God is about a power encounter. It is about the power of God defeating the power of the evil one. It is about forming a new type of community that lives by this power through the presence of the Spirit. It is about this new community continuing the work Jesus has begun.

Jesus demonstrated that the evil one's power does not have dominion. This was made clear in the parables, demonstrated in the miracles, and confirmed in the numerous occasions when demons were cast out. The final demonstration of the power of God came with the resurrection of Jesus from the dead. Even death, the great sting of the evil one, was defeated in the power encounter (1 Cor. 15:26). With this final defeat, the good news of the forgiveness of sins and reconciliation with God could be announced to the world. This leads to some important implications for the church in relation to the kingdom of God.

## Jesus Anticipates the Church

The word church is only used twice in the Gospel accounts, both times in Matthew. While these uses of the term are usually ascribed to later developments in the early Christian community to which Matthew was writing, it is clear in the Gospels that Jesus fully anticipated the development of an ongoing community of followers.[9] This is most evident in his careful selection and training of the twelve apostles who were to serve as the foundational leaders of this new community. His work with the Twelve offers some insights into the relationship of the church to the kingdom.

### The Little Flock

In teaching the Twelve about the character of the kingdom of God, Jesus identified the relationship between the kingdom and his followers who were to become the church (Luke 12:22–40). He noted the hardship they would encounter as well as the care the Father would provide. In the midst of this teaching, Jesus said, "Do not be afraid, little flock, for it is your Father's good pleasure to give you the kingdom" (32). What does this promise tell us about the relationship of Jesus' followers to the kingdom?

First, Jesus saw his followers as a "little flock." They were the fulfillment of the Old Testament expectation of a new people who would worship the living and true God. This "little flock" was the foundation upon which God would develop the new

84

Israel. The church is the extension of this little flock, built on the foundation of the apostles. The kingdom of God anticipates and calls into existence a people of God, the church. The church comes into existence and is shaped by the reality of God's redemptive reign.

Second, this "little flock" was a prototype church. Called into existence by the kingdom, it was also to receive this kingdom. While all creation is to be redeemed, the redemptive power of God's reign is manifested most directly in and through the church. This reflects God's good pleasure. The great power encounter between God's redemptive reign and the forces of evil will be played out in the church's relationship with the world. This missionary posture of the church toward the world is confirmed later in Paul's teaching that "through the church the manifold wisdom of God is now made known to the principalities and powers in the heavenly places" (Eph. 3:10).

## "I Will Build My Church"

When Jesus asked the Twelve who they believed he was, this gave occasion for Peter's great confession (Matt. 16:13–20). Peter's affirmation "You are the Messiah, the Son of the living God" (16) provided opportunity for Jesus to teach about his coming crucifixion and about the new community that was to be formed. This teaching gives several insights into the relationship between the kingdom and the church.

First, confessional witness to Jesus' deity and purpose depends on the supernatural power of God. "Blessed are you, Simon. . . . For flesh and blood has not revealed this to you, but my Father in heaven" (17). It is God who fosters faith.

Second, such witness will serve as a foundation in the formation of the church. "On this rock," says Jesus, "I will build my church" (18). The community of faith is formed by Jesus, belongs to him, and will be built by him.

Third, the church will stand strong in the world: "The gates of Hades cannot prevail against it" (18). This image of the gates

85

of Hades parallels the teaching about the strong man being bound. The church is to take the offensive, taking on the enemy and reclaiming lost territory. The church is to be missionary in nature, participating in the great mission of God's redemptive reign confronting the forces of evil.

Fourth, the church will have the "keys of the kingdom" (19). These keys give the community of faith, the church, the authority to loose and bind. This image parallels Jesus' teaching that it is the Father's good pleasure to give the kingdom to the little flock. The loosing and binding is not some arbitrary authority the church takes upon itself; it is the dynamic, redemptive presence of God at work in and through the church. As the church bears witness to Jesus, persons come to a right relationship with God. The church, the community of God's people in the world, is the place where faith is formed and forgiveness of sins is extended. The church stands at the crossroads between God and the world.

While the authority to forgive sins is God's alone, the church has been entrusted with the responsibility to exercise this authority in the world. The responsibility of this stewardship places tremendous importance on the new community being formed in Jesus' name. This makes it critical for Jesus' followers to understand the nature of this new community that the Spirit is creating in the world through his power.

## The Spirit as Advocate-Helper of the Community of Faith

During Jesus' celebration of the Passover, he tells his disciples how this community will be formed and how it will function (John 13–17). Jesus is about to leave the little flock on their own, but he is not going to leave them alone. He is going to send them the Spirit as their "Advocate-Helper" to lead them into truth and teach them all things (14:16, 26). This new community will relate to Jesus and the Father by the Spirit. It will experience the power of God's redemptive reign through the Spirit's presence.

The community of faith anticipated by Jesus will be created by the Spirit and participate fully in the great redemptive drama of God. The Spirit will "prove the world wrong about sin and righteousness and judgment" (16:8) as the redemptive reign of God engages the world. The Spirit's indwelling of the community of faith will be central to the church's being in mission to the world.

This great redemptive drama places the church center stage, but it does so in relationship to the larger framework of God's redemptive reign. The church does not establish the parameters of God's reign; the parameters of God's reign defines the role of the church. The church has not always gotten this sequence right.

## "Receive, Enter, Seek, and Inherit" versus "Build, Extend, Promote, and Establish"

It is interesting to listen to the words used to discuss the church's relationship to the kingdom of God. It is not uncommon to hear such concepts as "the church is responsible to build the kingdom of God," or "the church is to extend God's kingdom in the world," or "the church must promote the work of the kingdom of God," or "the church is to help establish God's kingdom in the world." These images of build, extend, promote, and establish stand in sharp contrast to the biblical language used to define the relationship of the church to the kingdom of God.[10]

The biblical language places emphasis on our response to God's redemptive reign. The words most commonly used are receive, enter, seek, and inherit. Jesus told his disciples, "Truly I tell you, whoever does not receive the kingdom of God as a little child will not enter it" (Luke 18:17). He noted how hard it is for someone who has material riches to enter the reign of God (18:24–25), but pointed out that those who left behind worldly comforts for the kingdom would receive much more in God's reign (18:29–30). Jesus taught that the central feature of being his disciple was to seek the kingdom of God as one's first priority in life (Matt. 6:33). Finally, faithful disciples would one day inherit the kingdom (Matt. 25:34).

The Church and the Redemptive Reign of God

These images are critical for comprehending the nature of the church, understanding its ministry, and shaping its organization. God's redemptive reign is offered as a gift to the community of faith. The church can receive this gift, can enter into it, must seek it, and will inherit it. These responses to the kingdom, however, are costly. God's reign divides natural affiliations (Luke 14:26; 16:16). It calls on people to leave the world's system of power and to enter into the power of God's redemptive reign. The world's system of power, under the control of the evil one, is not neutral. The powers will not let go easily. Forceful resistance is to be expected when the transfer of faith loyalties takes place.

The church does not possess God's reign, it is to be possessed by it. This makes the church an agent of the kingdom. Its nature, its very existence, stems from the presence of the kingdom. Its ministry, what it does, is an expression of God's redemptive work in the world. Its organizational life, how it structures itself, is shaped by its ministry and the power encounter taking place between the kingdoms.

God's redemptive work in the world has three aspects: creation, re-creation, and consummation. A closer look at each of these aspects can help us better understand the character of God's redemptive reign and in turn shed light on God's intent for the church's role in his redemptive work in the world.

## Creation, Re-creation, and Consummation

The outreach committee at St. Matthew Lutheran ELCA in Springdale was meeting to plan next year's ministry. To Sally, the chairperson, it was like a broken record, the same conversation over and over. About half of the committee wanted to stress what they called "socially responsible witness," addressing such issues as homelessness, adult literacy, and spouse abuse. The other half wanted to emphasize personal evangelism and reaching unchurched persons in their community.

Sally wondered, "Are there two gospels in the Bible, one that calls us to care about human hurts and another that calls people to reconcile their broken relationship with God? Can we ever get past playing one task against another?" After collecting her thoughts, she said to the committee, "We need to develop a more holistic understanding of the work of God in the world, and the role of the church in this work. What are some biblical starting points for helping us get past our dichotomy?"

The outreach committee at St. Matthew Lutheran is a microcosm of much of the church in North America. The battle lines between evangelism and social action have been sharply drawn between many churches, as well as within many churches. These lines are often drawn along perceived conservative and liberal theological positions. The debate that ensues often produces much heat but little light. The church in North America needs to reframe this discussion starting from a more holistic understanding of the work of God in the world.

The church is a people shaped by the redemptive reign of God. The church is not an end in itself. It has a distinct calling—to demonstrate the reality of God's redemptive power in the world. It has a unique nature—to live as a fellowship that demonstrates kingdom values and expresses kingdom power. It has a distinct purpose of carrying out a ministry of participating fully in the redemptive work of God in the world. The fuller implications of this become clearer when the kingdom of God and the church are placed in the context of creation design and God's consummation plan. In understanding God's works of creation, re-creation, and consummation, we can gain perspective on the larger issues associated with defining the nature, ministry, and organization of the church.

To understand God's purposes, we need to return to the biblical story. One of the most important aspects of this story relates to God's work relative to the presence of sin in the world. The biblical story has four unique chapters: Genesis 1–2 and Revelation 21–22. These chapters are unique in that no sin is present in the places and events described. Genesis 1–2 gives us a picture of God's creation design, what the world was like before sin entered the scene. Revelation 21–22 gives us a picture of God's future intent, what the world will be like once redemption has been fully completed with the consummation of the judgment of sin and the evil one.

These four chapters serve as bookends to the rest of the biblical story. The rest of the story is about the redemptive work of God in a sinful and fallen world. The story of re-creation relates the redemptive work of God to creation design by showing how he is restoring to right relationship that which was broken. This story of re-creation also relates the redemptive work to a consummation future of what a fully restored world will look like. It is the story of a community of faith formed by God as the place of his redemptive work in the world.

This story has two major phases. In the first phase, the Old Testament community of faith is looking forward to the fulfillment of the promise of redemption. In the second phase, the New Testament church has resulted from the full introduction of this redemption, even as it looks toward the final consummation.

A community of faith now lives between the times of the inauguration of the kingdom by Jesus and its final consummation. To understand what living between the times is to be like, we need to understand the frameworks of both creation design and re-creation redemption.

## Creation Design

"In the beginning God created the heavens and the earth" (Gen. 1:1). The Bible starts with this simple assertion and works from this premise throughout the rest of the story. The created world is the work of God. It was designed by God. It belongs to God. Everything in it finds its meaning and purpose in relationship to God. This is the key to understanding creation design.

All that is in the world exists in relationship to God. Exactly how, though, did God intend the created world to relate to him?

As figure 7 illustrates, Genesis 1–2 tells us a great deal about how creation design was to function.

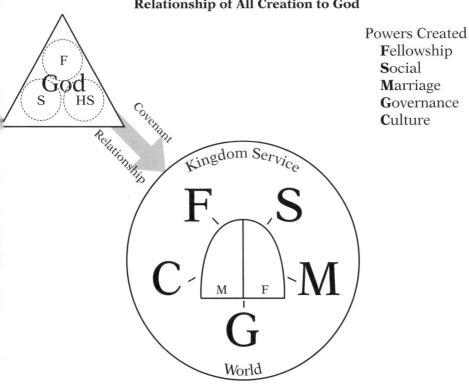

**Figure 7**

**Relationship of All Creation to God**

Powers Created
**F**ellowship
**S**ocial
**M**arriage
**G**overnance
**C**ulture

## Covenantal Relationship

God created the whole of the world in relation to himself. The most important truth built into God's design is that humans are to understand their existence as creatures before the living God, their creator. All of creation exists according to his purposes and for his glory. God gave a special place to humans within the creation, making them in his image and assigning them responsibility to exercise stewardship over the whole earth.

## Kingdom Service

"The earth is the Lord's and all that is in it" (Ps. 24:1). The world belongs to God. Therefore, in creation, human stewardship related to the whole of life. Every dimension of human existence was covered within this stewardship. All the created powers functioned as servants for making this stewardship possible. These created powers can be seen in the variety of responsibilities Adam and Eve were given in carrying out their stewardship.

## Fellowship

God created humans in his image, making them capable of relationships. Their most important relationship was to be with God himself. This fellowship was structured into creation both in the Sabbath principle of the seventh day of rest (2:2) and in the daily communion God had with Adam and Eve in the cool of the day (3:8). Humans were created to worship. This capacity was the most important of the created powers God entrusted to humans.

## Social

As a tri-unity, a social community exists within the Godhead. Humans, created in the image of God, were created social by nature (1:26). They were to live in community, come to understand their individual identity from community, and express their individuality through community. This capacity for community was also a created power.

## Marriage and Family

God created humans as male and female (1:27). Mutual attraction of men and women as complementary genders was another of the created powers (2:23–24). In this complementary relationship, men and women were to find intimacy, transparency, and fulfillment. They were also to give birth to children and raise them to form families (1:28). God's purpose was to create communities based on the building block of human families.

## Governance

Adam and Eve were given the responsibility to exercise their stewardship over all of creation through making decisions and exercising governance. They were to subdue the earth and establish dominion (1:28–30). They were to take the principle of the Garden of Eden and to extend its borders around the world—to "Edenize" the earth. This capacity to govern on behalf of God was another created power.

## Culture

Adam and Eve were placed in a garden that God had planted and were given responsibility to cultivate it (2:15). God also asked them to name the animals (2:19–20). Humans were to use both their physical and mental skills to form culture. Growth, development, and change were programmed into creation design. The capacity to create culture was another of the created powers.

## Sin and Redemption

When sin entered the story, everything changed. No relationship within creation design was left undamaged (see fig. 8).

Sin perverted the use of the created powers in every aspect of life. Fallen and rebellious angels in the heavenly realm stood against God's purposes. Humans worshiped gods made after their own likeness rather than the Creator God. Community was broken by betrayal, deceit, and murder. The intimacy of marriage rooted in human sexuality was disrupted by the corrupted powers of lust. Humans governed in a manner that exploited the earth and subdued other humans. All the cultural fruit of human effort was complicated by the presence and power of sin.

Sin was devastating. The fall was total. There was no hope for a solution within the human situation. But then, God promised a solution. A savior would come into the world as the "seed

## Figure 8

### The Impact of Sin on Creation Design

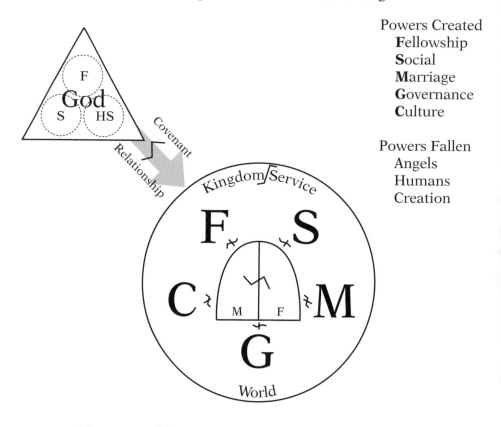

Powers Created
Fellowship
Social
Marriage
Governance
Culture

Powers Fallen
Angels
Humans
Creation

of the woman" (Gen. 3:15). This seed would ultimately conquer and defeat the seed of the evil one, crushing his head. This promise of a savior introduced the story of redemption. The anticipated coming of Jesus also introduced grace and the forgiveness of sins into this story.

These dynamics of a savior, grace, forgiveness of sins, and a redeemed seed are the core elements of the rest of the biblical story all the way to Revelation 21–22. All that varies is the form God used to convey this message to the world. In the Old Testament, after initially working through families, God chose one family to produce a nation for the purpose of demonstrating redemption to the world while preparing for the coming of the promised Messiah. In the New Testament, God fulfilled this promise by introducing a redemptive reign in the person and presence of Jesus.

With the crucifixion and resurrection as the cornerstone of this redemptive work, Jesus ushered in God's redemptive reign. Through this reign, God was bringing back to right relationship all that was lost. God was re-establishing creation design.

But something had changed. The creation design was being altered and would be transformed into a new reality, the new heavens and new earth. Here, the limits of human existence

**Figure 9**

**The Cross in Relation to Creation and Resurrection**

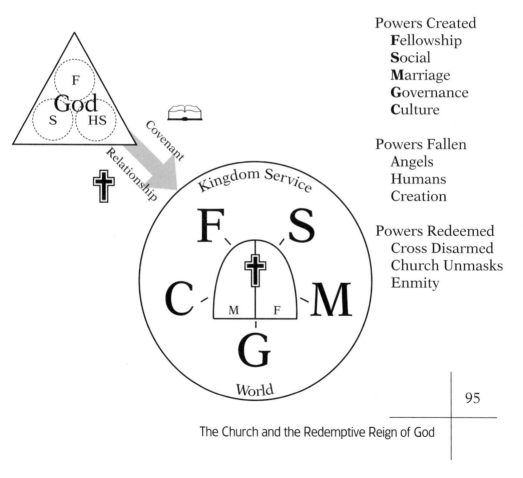

Powers Created
    **F**ellowship
    **S**ocial
    **M**arriage
    **G**overnance
    **C**ulture

Powers Fallen
    Angels
    Humans
    Creation

Powers Redeemed
    Cross Disarmed
    Church Unmasks
    Enmity

would be lifted. Through his announcement of the reign of God, Jesus made clear that this new reality of human existence had already begun. This new reality would be embodied in a new type of community, a community of faith. This new community of faith lived amidst a fallen community of humanity that still served the prince of the power of the air. There would be enmity between these two communities. Bridging the differences between them could only come on the basis of grace and redemption (see fig. 9).

The cross changed everything. To understand the cross, we must begin with creation. To understand creation, we must begin with the character of the Triune God.

## The Mission of God As Trinitarian and Eschatological

Foundational to understanding the nature, ministry, and organization of the church is understanding who God is and what God is like.

### The Mission of God As Trinitarian

The most important truth we can confess is that God is. God exists, and God's existence serves as the basis for us to understand the existence of the church. The church belongs to God. It possesses a new nature given to it by God. The church living out of this new nature demonstrates both the reality and the power of God.

In confessing that God is, we encounter God's existence as a trinity—a tri-unity, a social community of three persons within the Godhead. God's existence as a social community serves as the basis for us to understand the social nature of the church. The church is a relational community because God is a relational God. Because believers have been reconciled with God, they also must be reconciled with one another.

In confessing that God is, we also encounter the reality that God acts, that he is a sending, or missionary, God. God sent his Son into the world to accomplish redemption. The Father and Son sent the Spirit to create the people of God as a missionary people.

But this concept of a missionary God also needs to be viewed in relation to a prior act of God—creation. God created the heavens and the earth through the full participation of the Son and the agency of the Spirit. It is this same creation, now fallen, that God seeks to redeem. The entire Godhead—Father, Son, and Spirit—are dynamically involved in the mission of God within creation, re-creation, and the final consummation.[11]

The Father's work is expressed most fully in the Bible in terms of the plan and design of creation, re-creation, and consummation. The decision to create, the plan to restore creation to its rightful relationship, and the revealing in the end of the new heavens and new earth are all related to the glory of God within the purposes of the Father.

The Son's work is expressed most fully in the Bible in terms of accomplishing the purposes and plans of the Father. The act of creating, the inauguration of the kingdom reign of God, the accomplishment of redemption on the cross, being raised from the dead, and offering up to the Father the fullness of the kingdom in the end are all related to the work of the Son.

The Spirit's work is expressed most fully in the Bible as the agency for implementing the plan of the Father and the work of the Son. The formation of the initial creation, the forming of the church in relationship to God and empowering it for service in the world, and the indwelling of God's presence throughout the new heavens and earth are all related to the agency of the Spirit.

Mission is related to the sending work of God. The Son is sent by the Father. The Spirit is sent by the Father and the Son. To gain a proper view of the church we must understand that God is active in the world. The redemptive reign of God is dynamically leading the church into a power encounter with the forces of evil.

## The Mission of God As Eschatological

Just as important as understanding the trinitarian foundations for the mission of God is understanding its implications for the future. Fallen creation now looks toward a consummation of what was begun in the work of Christ, a work now carried forward by the Spirit.

The church lives between the times. For the church, heaven has already begun. The full redemptive power of God through the Spirit has entered time-space history. Jesus' inauguration of God's reign was the beginning of the end. The future is an accomplished fact, even though it is still unfolding in human history.

In a sinful world, the presence of the church demonstrates that heaven has already begun in terms of the presence and power of the Spirit in our midst. This is true even though sin has not yet been fully judged nor the power of evil removed. As a new humanity, the church is responsible to bring God's redeeming power to every dimension of life. It does so by confronting the powers of evil and bringing back to right relationship that which was lost. It does so through the grace and power of God that become evident through our weakness. This power in weakness comes from the same Spirit who led Jesus to live a life of suffering service. It is a power that can never be forced or legislated.

## The Church As Missionary by Nature

The church is missionary by nature because God has sent it on a mission in the world under the leading of the Spirit. It is to bear witness to God's redemptive reign. Just as God is a missionary God, so the church is to be a missionary church. It is to live fully within the active, redemptive, kingdom reign of God in the world as it is led and taught by the Spirit. It is to be a new community that expresses both the intent of creation design and the aspirations of re-creation as it anticipates the new heavens and new earth. This missionary nature of the church is captured in several images being used in current mission theology—the images of sign, foretaste, and instrument.[12]

This new community is to live as a sign to the world that the full redemptive reign of God is present in the world. Being a sign means that the very presence of the church in the world is a missionary statement by God. This new community is to live as a foretaste of this redemption, making available to everyone the fruit of grace-filled living. Being a foretaste means that every aspect of the life and ministry of the church in the world represents missionary activity. And this new community is to serve as an instrument to convey this Good News to others. It expresses this both in what it is and in what it does, both through its presence and its intentional acts. This concept of living as a new community invites the church to rethink and rediscover the biblical relationship between church and kingdom.

## God's Demonstration Plot

Growing up on a farm in rural Iowa provided me with an object lesson for understanding the church's being missionary by nature. Each county in the state employed an extension agent to work with farmers. These extension agents were usually university graduates with degrees in agriculture. As new farming technologies, seeds, and fertilizers became available, the extension agents introduced these to farmers. My dad, like many farmers, was often hesitant to accept the innovations. One of the methods extension agents used to gain acceptance of these innovations was demonstration plots.

A strip of land, usually along a major roadway, was selected as a demonstration plot, where a new farming method, seed, or fertilizer was used to raise a crop. It was not uncommon for farmers to remain skeptical throughout the summer as the crops grew. But there was always keen interest in the fall when the crop was harvested. Invariably, the innovation performed better than the crops in the surrounding fields. By the next year,

99

many farmers, including my dad, would be using the innovation as if it had been their idea all along.

The church is God's demonstration plot in the world. Its very existence demonstrates that his redemptive reign has already begun. Its very presence invites the world to watch, listen, examine, and consider accepting God's reign as a superior way of living.

# The Nature of the Church

The council meeting at Trinity Lutheran (LCMS) was getting tense. It was fall, the church was experiencing its annual shortfall in receipts, and the finance committee had just made its recommendations on how to cut expenses. They had suggested significant cuts in both staffing and programming. While this contributed to the tension, what had really gotten sparks flying was a comment made by Steve, the chair of the finance committee. "We need to run this church more like a business," he had said as he finished his report, "and we need to be more fiscally responsible. If the members don't want to pay for the services they receive, then we need to cut back on delivery of those services."

While no one disagreed with the need to be fiscally responsible, something about what Steve said didn't sit right with several council members. Bob started the discussion. "I don't think we should see the church as a consumer organization. I'm serving on this council because I believe in our mission, not because I'm receiving some service."

Dan joined in, "I agree. We need to help our people understand that this is their ministry, something we all share in together."

Paul then asked, "How do we get them to understand this?"

Pastor Robertson sat back and thought for a moment. "You know, I think we have something backward in our conversation. We are discussing what the church is supposed *to do*, and that's important. But maybe we need to step back and ask ourselves a deeper question. Maybe we should ask, 'What is the church supposed *to be?*'" The blank stares Pastor Robertson saw as he looked around the room told him that most council members were not used to thinking about the church in these terms.

What does it mean *to be* the church? This is the critical question for the church in North America to ask in the twenty-first century. Better management practices and improved organizational structures will carry churches only so far in addressing the changing mission context. While these can and should provide helpful contributions to a church's ministry, they are not sufficient for rethinking the church. Something more fundamental is required. We must understand what it is that God has created in forming the church.

## God's Redemptive Reign Introduced

Jesus laid the groundwork for the Spirit's creation of the church. He carefully selected a band of followers who would serve as the core leadership of this church. He recruited a broader following of disciples who would be among its first members. He taught the core beliefs that would shape this new community's identity and guide its ministry. He did all this as part of introducing God's redemptive reign on earth. Then before Jesus left his disciples, he promised to send the Spirit, the Spirit who would create the church.

As we move from the four Gospels to Acts, the focus shifts from God's redemptive reign as inaugurated by Jesus, to God's redemptive reign as implemented by the Spirit. In making this transition, it is helpful to summarize the key themes Jesus stressed regarding the character of God's redemptive reign.

This reign reflects creation design.
This reign anticipates the new heavens and new earth.
This reign defeated the principalities and powers.
This reign was demonstrated in Jesus' life and ministry.
This reign brings redeemed life to all the created powers.
This reign anticipated the church as creation of the Spirit.

The Nature of the Church

# God's Redemptive Reign Implemented

On the day of Pentecost, God poured out his Spirit on his followers gathered in Jerusalem, giving birth to the church. The large crowd of Jewish worshipers, many of them Gentile proselytes to Judaism, witnessed this event and heard Peter's sermon identifying what they were hearing and seeing as the fulfillment of Old Testament prophecy. That day thousands from many nations believed in Christ, becoming charter members of the church.

It is significant that this took place on the day of Pentecost, also known as the Feast of Harvest and the Day of Firstfruits. The occasion for this feast was the dedication of the firstfruits of the corn harvest. In choosing this day to pour out his Spirit, God was announcing that the church being born that day was the firstfruits of a great harvest that would fulfill the Old Testament expectation that through Israel, all nations would come to God.

There always was a people of God in redemptive history, a people who represented the "offspring" of the woman in the world who experienced enmity with the "offspring" of Satan (Gen. 3:15). This people of God received a national framework within the Abrahamic covenant, but God's intent was always for Israel to focus attention toward the nations. God's covenants with Israel were never intended to give Israel an exclusive relationship with God. These covenants were offered as a guarantee to both Israel and the world that God was not yet through with the world. Israel was always intended to be a blessing to the nations and a light to the Gentiles.

Through the Old Testament covenantal framework, God's plan of redemption was progressively revealed, always keeping in view all the nations and the whole of creation. The Pentecost event fulfilled the Old Testament promise that salvation was to be proclaimed freely and fully to everyone.

The birth of the church opened a new chapter in God's redemptive work. God's presence in the world would no longer be mediated through a single nation nor located in the physical Temple in Jerusalem. God was constructing a spiritual building consisting of people from all nations.

Other New Testament writers use this image of the church as the temple of God to express important truths about the nature of the church (see especially Paul in 1 Cor. 3:16–17 and Eph. 2:21–22). Jesus himself is the cornerstone, the stone that controls the design, determines the shape, and sets the parameters of the spiritual temple being built by the Spirit.

The apostles are the foundation of this spiritual temple. They bring two important dimensions to the formation of the church. One is their stewardship of Jesus' authority and teaching. The other is their responsibility to carry his message to the ends of the earth. The stones built into the temple are all those who come to faith in Christ. Christ joins them into a common community of faith, the church.

On the day of Pentecost, God began building this spiritual temple. Just as the cloud of God's presence invaded Solomon's temple (2 Chron. 7:1–3), so the presence of the Spirit was revealed to all who were gathered in Jerusalem. The Spirit's presence was observed in the sound of wind, the tongues of fire over the disciples' heads, and their speaking in other languages. The spiritual temple of God was being filled with the Spirit. God's redemptive reign was becoming visible in the world. The Spirit was creating the church.

The church is unlike any other community, social organization, or human institution that has ever existed. The church displays characteristics of being a community, organization, and institution, but it has a unique nature that makes it different. The first section of this chapter examines some of the names and images the New Testament writers employed in describing this new reality. The second section re-examines one of the more important historical confessions about the church by exploring further some of its implications for understanding the church today.

## The Church in the New Testament

The Book of Acts tells us that those whom the Spirit had formed into the church were known first as members of "the

Way" (9:2), and that in Antioch the "disciples were first called Christians" (11:26).[1] As the fuller reality of living within God's redemptive reign unfolded, this new community came to be called the *ecclesia,* which means "a called-out assembly." The Septuagint had used this word to translate the Hebrew word for the "people of God," although *synagogue,* which means "a gathering together," was more commonly used to describe the Jewish movement in Palestine.

One might have expected these early disciples to draw on their Jewish heritage by calling their new community something like a Christian synagogue. But the inclusive character of the church probably influenced the choice of terms. Uncircumcised Gentiles were not welcome in the synagogue. *Ecclesia* represented a more acceptable description. In the Hellenistic world, it was used to describe a political gathering, an official meeting of an assembly of citizens. This usage is found in Acts 19:29, where the town clerk cautioned the crowd that any official action toward Paul and his associates would have "to be settled in the regular assembly *[ecclesia]*."

## The Visible Church

The authors of the New Testament did not distinguish between the visible and invisible church. To them, the church that existed in the world was the only church there was. With all its sinfulness, brokenness, conflict, doctrinal heresy, and lukewarmness, the authors of the New Testament saw the visible church as the creation of the Spirit. This visible church was *the* church. Since the church possessed the Spirit, it was described by all the biblical attributes associated with being a spiritual community of faith. This approach motivated the early church to work zealously to bring the expectation of spiritual life within the reality of the human condition.

A case can be made for an invisible church.[2] The biblical message assumes there is a totality of all believers who have lived, who now live, or who will one day live are all part of the church of Jesus Christ. This conception of the church has some merit in understanding the redemptive work of God throughout the ages.

Profound problems are introduced, however, if it is argued that only such an invisible church possesses the true attributes of the church. Many streams of Protestant church life in North America, especially those identified with the evangelical tradition, have traditionally assigned such attributes as *one, holy,* and *catholic* to the invisible church only. This resulted from a desire to affirm their belief in the essential attributes of the church without having to insist on preserving such attributes in practice among the churches that actually existed.

This is not to deny the necessity of discerning when a church is no longer the church of Jesus Christ. But we do an injustice to the teaching of the New Testament authors if we impose this conception of an invisible church on the ideas they formulated. These authors were describing the concrete, historical, visible church that had come into existence in their day, and which was rapidly spreading throughout the Mediterranean world. It is this church that they chose to label the *ecclesia.*

The church as *ecclesia* was to live as a people whose existence and identity were shaped by God. God was the one who was calling this assembly together. God was the one who was creating this gathered community through the Spirit. But the church was left with the task of trying to explain its existence as a new type of human community in the world that was also holy. In doing so, numerous images were selected that are full of theological content and implications.

## Biblical Images of the Church

The New Testament uses multiple images to discuss the church. Many of these draw on Old Testament themes and metaphors. Some reflect the church's effort to define itself within the realities of first-century Jewish, Greek, and Roman cultures. Paul Minear in *Images of the Church in the New Testament* identified ninety-six images and analogies that are used in the New Testament to refer to the church.[3]

The writers of the New Testament did not try to synthesize or standardize these multiple images. They appear as a kaleidoscope of complementary perspectives. In different contexts

The Nature of the Church

the church naturally drew on different images for its self-understanding. This means that in the history of the church as well, different contexts would naturally influence the selection from the biblical record of images that would be used to explain the church in different periods of time.

This diversity of images reflects the truth that the church's nature, ministry, and organization is multifaceted. Some of the biblical images, such as "people of God" and "temple," relate mostly to the nature of the church. Others, such as "body of Christ" and "communion of saints," relate to both the nature and the ministry of the church. Few, however, suggest much about the organization of the church. This aspect of the church must be developed from other biblical materials.

In the West, we have tended to systematize biblical truth into a series of propositional statements. While such systematizing is helpful in gaining perspective on the whole teaching of Scripture, it risks depreciating the wide range of meanings conveyed through the multiple images. It can also lead to losing sight of the original context of the images, which hinders our ability to apply them to our own settings. The better approach is to treat all these materials as complementary, considering points of overlap as needed.

Minear points out that most of the images and analogies, while teaching us something about the church, are not central to understanding the essential nature of the church. But four frequently used core images do reveal essential aspects of this new community of faith created by the Spirit. New Testament writers used these images more frequently to make connections between the existence of the new community of faith and the explicit nature of this new community as the creation of the Spirit.

## Core Biblical Images of the Church

The core biblical images for the church all develop a common theme: the church is a social community.[4] These images help us understand that the visible church in the world, with all its organizational and institutional characteristics, is to be understood primarily as a social fellowship of persons. Comprehending this is crucial if we are to gain a proper perspective for understanding the nature of the church. The church is not a building. The church is not a set of organized programs and activities. The church is not just a collection of individuals. The church is not primarily a legitimization of authority lodged in an institution. The church is a social community, a community made up of people who are reconciled with God and one another.

To be the church is to be in reconciled relationship. To be the church is to be in active fellowship. To be the church is to live in interdependence with others. The church as social community reflects the social reality of the Trinity. The four primary images that depict the church as a social community are the people of God, the body of Christ, the communion of saints, and the creation of the Spirit.

## People of God

The image of the people of God makes direct and intentional connections with the Old Testament story. Peter uses a series of images to make this connection: "You are a chosen race, a royal priesthood, a holy nation, God's own people" (1 Peter 2:9). The church is pictured here as the New Testament fulfillment of Old Testament prophetic expectations regarding the people of Israel.

This new people, this spiritual Israel, finds its identity as God had always intended, along faith lines, not blood lines. It is formed by a common faith in the saving work of Christ, by the work of God himself. Paul notes this in applying the prophet Hosea's words, spoken to Israel, to the church now made up of both Gentiles and Jews: "Those who were not my people I will call 'my people,'. . . they shall be called children of the living God" (Rom. 9:25–26). This image has significant implications for the church.

The division of the world along racial or ethnic lines, and institutionalized into national, political units, will no longer exist within God's redemptive reign. For the people of God, there will be a new political reality. The people of God will be formed around a different identity, one that transcends race, ethnicity, and nationalism. It will be an identity rooted in a shared faith and fellowship with the living God. This new community will include people of diverse racial, ethnic, national, and political identities. This truth has profound implications for the church in a multicultural North America that is increasingly retribalizing.

It is the nature of the church to live in reconciled relationship with God and one another as a new "people of God." This message greatly challenged the Jewish Christians who had to learn to welcome Gentile Christians as full participants in the emerging community of faith. It is interesting that this image was not utilized much after the first century. Perhaps the obvious connections to the fulfillment of Old Testament expectations about Israel made it less useful in presenting the church to a largely Gentile audience. But in our day when life has become so politicized around ethnic, racial, and national identities, recovering this image in defining the nature of the church is important for bridging differences. Our fragmented world needs to see that a community of diverse persons can live in reconciled relationship with one another because they live in reconciled relationship with God.

In the midst of a divided world, the church must find ways to bridge differences as the "people of God." This different political reality for the church is implied in the choice of the term *ecclesia* to describe it. As mentioned earlier, in secular usage this term referred to those who were officially "called out and assembled" to conduct political business. There is a new political assembly in the world—the church. This new assembly has the spiritual power and biblical mandate to transcend all other political realities. The church, which is political by nature, lives by a political reality beyond the politics of the world. The church is to live visibly in the world as the newly created international people of God from "every tribe and tongue" (Matt. 28:19; Rev. 5:9–10). This has profound implications for understanding the ministry of the church in the world, as will be discussed in chapter 6.

## Body of Christ

One of the most popular images for the church as a social community is the body of Christ. This image has functioned within the North American church in recent years to emphasize spiritual gifts and small groups. It was developed most fully by Paul, especially in 1 Corinthians, Romans, Colossians, and Ephesians, but other New Testament authors also used it. The image of the human community as a body was a social-political idea current in Hellenistic circles in Paul's day.[5] Paul reformulates this organic image by relating it to the crucified, resurrected, and ascended Christ.

In relating it to the crucified Christ, Paul connects our partaking of the sacrament of the cup and bread with our participation in the suffering and death Jesus experienced in his body. "The bread that we break, is it not a sharing in the body of Christ? Because there is one bread, we who are many are one body, for we all partake of the one bread" (1 Cor. 10:16–17). The church becomes united as one body through partaking in the sacrament of the crucified body of Christ. The nature of the church entails a unity that transcends diversity. This unity is rooted in the sacrificial death of Christ and our common participation in this sacrifice. The church as the body of Christ is to live as a unified community in sacrificial love and fellowship.

In relating this image to the resurrected Christ, Paul describes our being united in the body of Christ as the work of the Spirit, creating a new humanity. This new humanity functions as the body of Christ on earth under Christ's headship through the ongoing work of the Spirit who gifts, guides, and graces the church. "For as in one body we have many members, and not all the members have the same function, so we, who are many, are one body in Christ, and individually we are members one of another" (Rom. 12:4–5). This means the nature of the church entails an interdependence among all the members. This interdependence is a function of the diversity of spiritual gifts that have been given by the Spirit for ministry by members. The church as the body of Christ is to live as a new community in dynamic, gift-shaped interdependence.[6]

The Nature of the Church

In relating it to the ascended Christ, Paul uses the image of the body to Christ as the divine ruler who is head over the church. "And [God] has put all things under [Christ's] feet and has made him the head over all things for the church, which is his body, the fullness of him who fills all in all" (Eph. 1:22–23). The church, while earthly and human, is also spiritual and plays an important role in God's cosmic plan. The church is a full participant in the power encounter between God's reign and the forces of evil. The church must never allow the powers of this world to seduce it into comfortable living, or into building earthly kingdoms. The battle is cosmic in scope and conflictive in character. Paul's use of this image of Christ's headship is closely related to the conception of God's redemptive reign. To be "in Christ" is to be within the redemptive reign of God that is both already and not yet.

## Communion of Saints

One biblical image for the church that has been used extensively over the centuries is the communion of saints. It appears in the Apostles' Creed: "I believe a holy catholic church, the communion of saints. . . ." It is interesting that these two ideas appear together without any explicit connection being made between them, such as, "I believe a holy, catholic church which is the communion of saints." While the concept of communion of saints was picked up by various theologians and confessions in the development of ecclesiology, other attributes usually took precedence.

This lack of development is unfortunate. The concept of the communion of saints appears frequently in the New Testament and is foundational for understanding the church. The term communion is a translation of *koinonia,* which refers to what we share in common (from *koine*—common). In our present English usage, *koinonia* is better translated as "fellowship." The essential idea of the church as a fellowship of saints is that we now experience God and each other in reconciled relationships based on what we share in common in Christ. These reconciled relationships lead to a kind of fellowship among believers that only persons of faith can experience.

The word fellowship is used with a number of other terms: fellowship of the Son (1 John 1:3, 6), fellowship of the blood of Christ (1 Cor. 10:16), fellowship of the Spirit (2 Cor. 13:14), and fellowship in the gospel (Phil. 1:5). The focus in all these passages is the same. God in Christ has brought into existence a new type of human community—a fellowship. "God is faithful; by him you were called into the fellowship of his Son, Jesus Christ our Lord" (1 Cor. 1:9).

The condition of being in fellowship is something God does, not something that we bring about. God through the Spirit has created this communion of saints. It is not an organized program. It is not a managed technique. It is not a personal choice. It is not an option. Being in fellowship means that the church by nature exists as a social community. The very existence of the church demonstrates to the world the truthfulness of the gospel of grace, forgiveness, and reconciliation. As will be discussed in chapter 6, this characteristic of the church has significant implications for the church's ministry.

## Creation of the Spirit

Jesus taught his followers that when he left them, another would come to be their Advocate-Helper. This Advocate-Helper is the Spirit of God, sent to indwell the community of faith with the fullness of God's presence and power. During the Reformation, Protestant churches tended to emphasize the work of the Spirit in the life of the individual believer. This emphasis was reinforced later through influences from Enlightenment thinkers.[7] While the calling, saving, sealing, gifting, and empowering works of the Spirit can be developed biblically from the perspective of the individual, this is not the New Testament's primary focus in defining the relationship between the Spirit and the church. The Bible's focus is not on individual Christians but on the formation of a new type of community, a new humanity that is indwelt by the Spirit.

The Nature of the Church

This corporate reality of God's work in salvation needs to be highlighted in relation to the church's nature. Many New Testament images bear witness to the inherently corporate character of the church: holy temple, dwelling place of God (1 Cor. 3:16; Eph. 2:19), living stones built into a spiritual house (1 Peter 2:5), members of the household of God (Eph. 2:19), and citizens with the saints (Eph. 2:19). This rich imagery provides several key insights for understanding the church's nature.

First, these images show that the church by nature is always in process. Stones are still being laid into the spiritual temple. Members are still being added to the household. Citizens are still becoming part of the new nation. This process began at Pentecost, has continued through the ages, and will continue until Christ returns to usher in the new heavens and new earth. These images indicate that it is the nature of the church to grow in both its spiritual life and its size. The church will expect, seek, and nurture this growth if it is living consistent with its nature.

Second, these images suggest that the church by nature will exhibit characteristics of organizational and institutional life. The visibility of the church in the world as a corporate social entity is inevitable. We would expect the various organizational and institutional expressions of the visible church to reflect the patterns of society within which the church develops.

As the church has reflected on these biblical images through the centuries, it has developed various theological descriptions of the church. We will look next in some detail at one of the most important of these.

## Historical Descriptions of the Church

Fellowship Community decided early in its life in the 1980s to make small groups of twelve to fifteen people their primary vehicle for discipling adults. This ministry had worked fairly well, and over sixty percent of the members were regularly participating in the twice-monthly meetings. All the groups studied the same Scripture passage each time they met. This week's study titled "The Oneness of the Church" explored Ephesians 4:1–6.

In preparing for the study, Sally wondered, "What does it mean that the church is one?" This could spark some interesting discussion in her group—a group consisting of two former Methodists, a former Episcopalian, three former Baptists, two former Presbyterians, and four with no denominational background. She smiled as she thought, "I'll bet we get into some real discussion when we get to verse 5—'one Lord, one faith, one baptism.'"

The actual discussion surprised her a little. Most of the members readily agreed that the oneness of the church was something that could only be experienced "in Christ," in what Robert referred to as the "invisible church."

But Mary, a former Episcopalian, took a different position. "I believe we need to think of the oneness of the church in more concrete terms, as something the world can see."

Ralph reacted to this with, "You know what happened when the ecumenical movement tried that. They sold out the gospel and got involved in all kinds of social-political agendas. That's one reason I left the Methodist church."

But Mary didn't back off. "No," she said, "I'm not talking about oneness of organization, but I do believe there is some sense in which God intends Christians to be unified in the world." The group tended to agree with her, but could offer little help in imagining what this unity might look like.

This discussion is not uncommon among many Christians in North America. How are we to think about the oneness of the church? Doing so requires that we think about the nature of the church. And when we do this, we are helped by some of the developments in ecclesiology over the centuries.

The Nicene Creed, originally articulated by the Council of Constantinople in 381, contains the phrase, "I believe one holy catholic and apostolic church." This list of the church's attributes is still relevant for reflecting on the nature of the church. Several points, however, should be noted about their development and historical use.

First, these attributes were formulated shortly following the establishment of the Christian faith as the official religion of the Roman Empire. The Christian church at that time was, in fact, one church, a single institution. The church was also seen as catholic, which simply meant it was universal. Since this empire took in most of the known world, the presence of the church was universal in this world. The church was considered holy because it was the creation of God. This attribute too described the church as a visible historical institution. The church was described as apostolic to legitimate its authority. The authority of the church was rooted in its carrying on the true teaching of the apostles. This true teaching was secured by tying it to the office of the bishop, an office seen as the legitimate extension of the authority of the apostles. The church's being one, holy, catholic, and apostolic all seemed self-evident to the bishops who met in Constantinople in 381.[8]

Second, all these attributes relate directly to New Testament teachings about the visible church in the world. As noted earlier, many in the Protestant tradition have applied these attributes only to the invisible church. This robs these attributes of their historical relevance. Other Protestants have continued to apply the attributes to the visible church, but have applied them narrowly to only the institutional church where the marks of pure preaching and the proper administration of the sacraments are present. This approach tends to treat these essential attributes not as characteristics the Spirit gives to the church, but as characteristics the church demonstrates by certain activities. Both approaches have limited the understanding of the church as a social community. In Catholic circles, this idea of the church being primarily a social community began to be recovered in Vatican II with the theology of the church as "people of God."

Third, some scholars suggest that the Nicene Creed presents these attributes as something that we believe, "And I believe one holy catholic and apostolic church." The rendering of the text, they argue, was "And I believe. . . ." rather than, "And I believe in. . . ." This is used to make a key point.[9] It is suggested that the bishops who shaped this confessional statement understood that the church they were confessing was not something that existed beyond them. It was not something they were responsible to construct. The church existed. The church existed by the act of God's work through the Spirit. This church was to be accepted and experienced as one, holy, catholic, and apostolic. This is important to reflect on in considering the nature, ministry, and organization of the church. The church belongs to God. It is the creation of the Spirit. We become a part of the church by the gracious work of God that we receive as a gift. The church is the center point of our new identity. We are a people who live as a corporate new humanity. Our primary identity is to be both spiritual and corporate. As such, we must learn to recover the affirmation that "I believe one, holy, catholic, and apostolic church."

Fourth, these four attributes, while biblically valid, do not necessarily say all that needs to be said about the nature of the church. Some have identified other attributes, while others have suggested more complete definitions for these four ideas. What follows takes the latter approach in laying the foundation for discussing the church's ministry and organization. The historical meaning of each of the four attributes is matched with a parallel idea that provides a fuller explanation for comprehending the nature of the church.

## Both Holy and Human, Spiritual and Social

The attribute of the church being holy speaks most directly to the reality that the church is the creation of the Spirit. To confess this attribute as essential to the nature of the church raises an important question. When we encounter sin, brokenness, and disobedience in the church, in what sense can we think of it as holy? As noted earlier, some have tried to resolve this tension by making holiness an essential characteristic of the invisible church only. This approach, however, violates the intent of the biblical images. It is the visible church that is holy. But what exactly does this mean?

### More Than Human

First, there is more to the church than meets the eye. The church is not just another social organization or human institution. While it has organizational and institutional dimensions, it is more than just the sum of these. The church is the creation of the Spirit. God's divine power and presence indwell the people of God. This makes the church a spiritual community as well as a human community. The church is both a spiritual reality and a sociological entity. It has divine roots in the eternal purposes of God, yet exists as a historically conditioned organization. It is both holy and human, both spiritual and social.

In understanding the holiness of the church we need to recognize that the "holiness of the church does not stem from its members and their moral and religious behavior."[10] The issue is not who we are as humans, but rather what God has done in bringing the church into existence. The redemptive reign of God, present through the indwelling of the Spirit, makes the church holy by nature. Just as God justifies individual believers and gives them a new nature, so also God creates the church through the Spirit and gives it a holy nature. It is a nature that is to display the reality of sanctification, a sanctification that is framed first and foremost in corporate terms.

God expects the church to be holy because God is holy. "You shall be holy, for I am holy" (1 Peter 1:16). The Bible presents this holiness as both a position we have received and as a process we continuously engage in. The church's holiness is the work of God through the Spirit on our behalf. Holiness is something the church already possesses because God gives it to the church as a gift. Holiness is also something the church continues to pursue because God calls the church to the task of living into and out of the full power of the gift it has received. This is what makes the church more than human. The church is to accept this gift of God's holiness and bring its life into obedient conformity with it.

## Living out of a Dual Nature

Second, it is important to understand how the church is to live out of its dual nature. Some discuss the holiness of the church by contrasting it with the church's sinfulness. They view the church as both holy and sinful. This approach, while descriptively true, misses the main point of the duality of the church's nature. The issue is not that the church is holy and sinful, but that the church is both holy and human. In its humanness, the church is to demonstrate the full possibilities of redeemed living in its visible, earthly, historical existence. That is what the invasion of God's redemptive reign into human history is all about.

Even though the church is more than human, it is also human. In all its ministry expressions, the church must seek to live out the attribute of holiness in concrete ways. In its organization, the church must live out its dual nature as both holy and human by structuring itself as a faithful covenantal community. The church, living this way, is profoundly missional. Living in covenantal relationship with God and one another requires more than a personal choice to be a committed member. It requires the transforming power of God working through the agency of the Spirit.

The holiness of the church is a work of the Spirit. It is the Spirit's power that indwells the community and its members. It is the Spirit who draws, leads, guides, teaches, counsels, and provokes the church into living by a redeemed set of values. This shared life of the Spirit means that the church is to organize its life together in the shape of intentional communities. Being intentional means these communities will practice the disciplines of redeemed living through the leading and power of the indwelling Spirit.

## Both Catholic and Local, Universal and Contextual

When the authors of the Nicene Creed said the church is catholic, they meant that the church extended throughout the known world. As a creation of the Spirit, the church is not limited by time and place, nor is it tied to any one social or political system. As the catholic, or universal church, created by the Spirit, the church transcends these limits. There are two aspects of catholicity that need to be understood. One relates to a contribution in recent years to mission theology on contextualization.[11] This emphasis notes how the church seeks to find its contextual relationship to every particular culture. The other relates to the understanding of the mission of God inaugurated by Jesus as God's redemptive reign. This emphasis notes how the church finds commonality within the multiple cultures of the world.

## Local As Contextual and Relevant

The church lives within the context of culture and is, therefore, always contextual. Jesus demonstrated the importance of contextualization in the incarnation. Just as the Word became flesh, so also the church is enfleshed in human cultures as the body of Christ. The church being enfleshed within culture means that the church by nature is to be contextual in every particular setting in which it exists. It has the inherent capacity to fit into every culture, to be relevant within the organizational and institutional dimensions of any context. This is part of what it means that the church is catholic. But as it exists in specific contexts, it is more than just another social organization or human institution; it is the agent of God in the world.

Like the Bible, the church through the Spirit is inherently translatable into every specific, cultural context.[12] In missiological circles this contextual translation is understood to be a necessary part of the missionary task. The church's capacity to be contextualized, to be made relevant to any and every cultural setting, is a logical extension of the confession that the church is catholic.

## Catholic As Universal and Normative

The contextualization of the church within any particular culture is not a neutral activity. Culture is not a passive configuration of puzzle pieces waiting for us to find the right alignment. A war is being waged against God in every cultural setting. The created powers, designed by God to give direction, meaning, and fulfillment to every area of life, are now fallen and serve the forces of evil as powers that enslave all human communities.

God's redemptive reign confronted these fallen powers. The usurpation of these created powers by the forces of evil was defeated in the work of Christ on the cross. Here, the powers were fully "disarmed" and made to be a "public example" of humiliation (Col. 2:15). The church continues this redemptive work of God by unmasking the powers that have already been defeated. It does this by exposing the powerlessness of the fallen powers in the face of God's power. Such unmasking calls the church to follow the method employed by Jesus of living as a suffering servant. Our confession that the church is catholic means that the church is the means by which the now defeated powers are confronted and unmasked. In this confrontation, the cultures of the world are made relative, the power of Satan is made ineffective, and the fallen powers are redeemed for their proper use within God's redemptive reign.

No human construction of social existence, whether rooted in racial identity, ethnic make-up, social-economic status, or political ideology can claim ultimate authority in the face of the catholicity of the church. The church, because of its catholic nature, makes an open declaration to the fallen powers that God reigns and has ultimate authority in heaven and on earth. The church's catholic nature anticipates the end of time when Christ will deliver the kingdom to the Father, and every knee will bow and every tongue confess that Jesus Christ is Lord (1 Cor. 15:24–25; Phil. 2:9–11).

## Both One and Many, Unified and Diverse

The unity of the church is a hard attribute for many in the church to confess today. This is because of the great diversity among Christian churches, many of which came into existence through conflict with others. When the bishops in Constantinople made this confession, the church existed throughout

The Nature of the Church

the world as one church. The bishops were describing a physical reality as much as making a theological statement.

With the breakup of the Medieval church during the Reformation, the confession of the church's being one went through some reformulation. The idea developed that there was a mystical oneness in the invisible church, a spiritual oneness that operated through the Spirit beyond the institutional church. This approach, however, loses something essential in understanding the church as the creation of the Spirit. Our approach to the church's oneness must come to terms with and within the complex diversity of the historical church.

## Many While Being One

In trying to understand the church as one, another reality needs to be affirmed: the church is also many. As with the attribute of holiness, some have proposed contrasting the church's oneness with its brokenness. The church is viewed as being one spiritually, but divided and conflictive in its historical expressions. This condition is accepted as inevitable and, for the most part, unresolvable. It is not uncommon for this approach to be advanced by those seeking to define a true church over against a false church. This further complicates the issue of what constitutes the church's oneness.

Rather than contrasting the church's oneness with its brokenness, it is more helpful to see its unity in conjunction with its diversity. That is, the church, while existing as one, also must exist as many.

The oneness of the church is a corollary to the church's being catholic. Just as the church is both catholic and local, both universal and contextual, the one church is contextual and relevant to diverse cultural settings. Of necessity, local churches take different forms. Such diversity is consistent with the church's catholic nature. It is also consistent with the church's oneness. This calls on the church to allow freedom in forms and styles while maintaining a common fellowship and confession. This calls on the church to learn to bridge the diversity it encounters by living into a biblical understanding of the oneness of the church.

## Oneness in the Midst of Diversity

The essential oneness of the church, its unity being demonstrable within time-space history, finds its source in the oneness of the Triune God. Jesus prayed "that they may be one, as we are one" (John 17:22). God invites redeemed humanity into a oneness that is to reflect fully the oneness of the Godhead. The church receives this oneness as a gift.

The starting point for thinking about the church is to recognize that it is already a community that possesses an essential oneness. In working from this starting point, it is as if God says to the diversity of churches in any context, "You are one. Now learn how to affirm each other's distinctiveness while you work out your differences." The character of our relationship with God, which is by necessity a oneness, requires a oneness in our relationships with each other. The social context of the church is to be treated as sacred space. Every part of the church must be zealous for the life, health, vitality, and unity of the whole.

The oneness of the church is not optional. It is a gift from God that must be expressed within the historical church. This does not necessarily require some type of organizational or institutional oneness. But it does mean that there needs to be a real communion of the saints among diverse expressions of the church in any particular setting. This communion may take a wide variety of forms, but the form is not the critical issue. What is critical is that the church must maintain its unity. Every church body must have the conviction and desire to relate to other church bodies that are part of the catholic church. To do less, according to Jesus, is to betray both the nature of God and the nature of the church. This has profound implications for the church in North America that exists as multiple denominations, mission structures, and local congregations. These will be explored in more detail in chapter 7.

# Apostolic: Both Foundational and Missionary, Authoritative and Sent

The apostolic nature of the church is one of the most important, yet one of the most difficult of the four Nicene attributes to define. The concern of the bishops at Constantinople was to secure the continuity of an apostolic tradition in relation to both authority and teaching.[13] The bishops believed that continuity for both the authority and teaching of the apostles came through the office of bishop. The bishop's office, passed on through the laying on of hands within the established church, gave the church historical continuity. The bishop's office was a teaching office to safeguard the content of teaching. It was also a governing office, with authority to oversee congregations and ministries within a diocese. The bishop exercised control over both teaching content and the church's organizational life.

This application of the apostolic attribute has powerfully influenced the history of the church. This is true not only in the Roman Catholic Church, but also in other traditions that retained the bishop's office as foundational to church polity, including Orthodox, Anglican-Episcopal, and Methodist.

The early Reformers saw the positing of apostolic authority in the bishop's office as part of the problem, especially the way this was used to legitimize the papal office as the rightful extension of Peter's apostolic authority. The confessional statements of these Reformers included affirmations of the church's being one, holy, and catholic, but they tended to downplay the apostolic attribute. This introduced some fundamental problems into our understanding of the nature of the church. Two aspects of the apostolic attribute need to be developed.

## The Foundational–Authoritative Aspect of the Apostolic Attribute

It is clear that the twelve men Jesus selected as his apostles were to function in foundational ways within the church that

123

would be created by the Spirit. Jesus gave some profound privileges to those twelve apostles. He gave them authority to proclaim the gospel message (Mark 3:14). He gave them authority to cast out evil spirits (Mark 3:15). He gave them the keys to the kingdom to make heavenly commitments in binding and loosing on earth (Matt. 16:19). He gave them protection and power for their responsibilities in participating in the formation of the church (John 17:6–19). He promised them great reward for making special sacrifices to follow him (Matt. 19:29). He promised that they would sit on twelve thrones in heaven to judge the twelve tribes of Israel (Matt. 19:28).

These incredible responsibilities and privileges were affirmed by other New Testament authors, especially Paul. Paul wrote that the church was built "upon the foundation of the apostles and prophets" (Eph. 2:20). He added that it was to the "holy apostles and prophets" that the mystery of God's reign was now revealed (3:5). Paul clearly saw himself as part of the apostolic order, both in terms of his message and his ministry, even though he was selected as an apostle after Jesus' earthly ministry was completed.

It is beyond the scope of this brief discussion to formulate all that can be said of the purpose and role of the apostolic office. But the Bible makes clear that the work of the apostles was foundational to forming the church. Their foundational work included both teaching and leading. The apostles' teaching guided the church through its transition from Jesus' inauguration of God's redemptive reign to the Spirit's creation of a visible church throughout the Mediterranean world. They also exercised their authority for ministry and governance to give shape to the church being created by the Spirit. Both the content of the church's message and operations of its ministry were founded on and shaped by the apostles.

The church's being apostolic by nature means it has been given stewardship of both the gospel message and of the organizational development of the church. God's authority is made visible in the church through the message it conveys to the world. It is also made visible through the structures and processes through which it carries out its ministry.

This authority is divine. This authority is apostolic. This authority continues in the church throughout the ages. This authority is communal. This authority is located in the visible church. This authority is mediated through human leaders. This authority is institutional. The church that is by nature apostolic must, of necessity, also be institutional. The critical task for the church is to live out this institutional reality, not as an end in itself, but under the leading and teaching of the Spirit within the mission of God in the world.

## The Missionary-Sent Aspect of the Apostolic Attribute

The other aspect of the church's being apostolic is its "sentness." The church is missionary by nature, created by the Spirit to participate fully in the redemptive reign of God. The very existence of the church in the world creates a missionary condition. All that the church does in living its life and in carrying out its ministry is missionary by intent. The church is missionary by nature because God through the Spirit calls, creates, and commissions the church to communicate to the world that the redemptive reign of God has broken into human history.

The church's being missionary by nature is an essential aspect of the attribute of the church's being apostolic. The basic definition of apostle is "sent one."[14] The apostles were sent to take the message of God's redemptive reign to the ends of the earth, making disciples of all nations. The sentness of the church is rooted in the apostolic ministry given to the original Twelve. Every community that becomes a part of the church inherits this sentness.

This sentness is to be the primary dimension of the apostolic attribute. The institutional dimensions of the church, those related to its teaching content and governance, are to support and mobilize the ministry of sentness.

In the history of the church, these two aspects of the apostolic attribute have often been inverted. Ministry has sometimes been defined as a function of an ordained office. A focus on who has the credentials and proper authority to do ministry has at times overshadowed the work of ministry itself. And rather than the organization of the church serving to mobilize members into ministry, all too often the members have been expected to serve the organization. This reverses the biblical order. The church's teachings and structures are intended to empower ministry.

Only by rightly understanding the nature of the church can we develop a proper understanding of its ministry and organizational life. The church's nature is rooted in God's purposes in creation and redemption. The church is created by the Spirit, the result of the Spirit's implementation of God's reign in human history.

Biblical teaching and theological reflections throughout the history of the church have given us a rich understanding of the essential characteristics of the church's nature. It is this nature of the church that serves as the foundation for understanding the ministry of the church, which is the theme of chapter 6.

# The Ministry of the Church

It was Friday evening, and the crowd was gathering at Springdale Assembly of God (AOG). About six months ago, a few members of the church had started getting together to pray for the ministry of their church in the community. Within a few months, the number of people coming grew to over one hundred. With the pastor's urging, this prayer meeting was turned into an informal service under the name River of Life with an emphasis on spiritual healing and spiritual warfare. Stories of people being "slain in the Spirit" soon spread into the community. By the sixth month, this service had grown to over three hundred people, with over one-half coming from other Springdale area churches.

This caused no little stir among some of the area pastors. At the monthly pastor's brown-bag lunch, attended mostly by pastors of mainline churches, the conversation turned to the River of Life service at Springdale AOG. Pastor Bill from Rockhill Baptist (USA) wanted to dismiss the whole phenomenon as one more version of people seeking after some emotional experience. Pastor Sharon from Asbury United Methodist, reported that several of her members were participating, and that some seemed to have experienced genuine healing of personal brokenness. While cautious, she didn't want to dismiss too quickly what was taking place.

Father Rodgers from St. Mary's Catholic entered the conversation at this point. "We've been doing spiritual healing services at St. Mary's for a number of years. Many of our people have really been strengthened in their spiritual journey. While I'm not sure about being 'slain in the Spirit,' I do know that a number of exorcisms have taken place."

Pastor Jim from Springdale Presbyterian (USA) summed up the feelings of several in the group: "For many of us, it seems like our seminary training on the work of the Spirit didn't adequately prepare us to relate to what is happening today."

The person and work of the Spirit is attracting greater attention in North American churches. Many congregations are reporting new spiritual energy from this emphasis. But not everything being done in the name of the Spirit is readily appreciated by other churches. How are we to understand the person and work of the Spirit within a trinitarian understanding of mission?

## The Church Does What It Is

Because the church is the creation of the Spirit, its ministry is a work of the Spirit. The church's ministry flows naturally out of its nature. This means that the church does what it is. The characteristics of this nature were presented in the last chapter. It is helpful to summarize the key elements of the church's nature that have a direct bearing on the church's ministry.

The nature of the church is defined by the mission of God in the world.

The nature of the church is the result of the redemptive work of Christ.

The nature of the church is holistic in relating this redemption to all of life.

The church exists as a social community that is both spiritual and human.

The church exists as a full demonstration of a new humanity.

The attributes of the church's nature determine the church's ministry.

This chapter develops an understanding of the ministry of the church in light of the nature of the church. First, how is the

*review*

*overlay*
*primary*
*images*

ministry of the church related to God's redemptive purposes? Second, what are the spiritual dynamics of ministry? And third, how does the church's identity as a community of God's people shape its ministry? While this discussion relates to the church in general, specific attention will be given to the ministry of local congregations.

## The Church's Ministry and the Mission of God

The church's ministry is often approached from the perspective of Christ, the cross, and the individual believer. This stems, in part, from developments during the Protestant Reformation.[1] At that time, to counteract perceived abuses of the Roman Catholic Church, attention was focused on the work of Christ on the cross and individual salvation.

The Reformers sought to address two primary problems. One was the continued use of the sacrament of communion to implement the sacrifice of Christ as the basis of salvation. The other was the control of this means of salvation through the priestly ministry of the institutional church.

To counter these practices, Protestants emphasized that the work of Christ had completed salvation once for all. They taught that because of the cross this salvation was available as a gift of grace. This gift of salvation was received by the faith response of the individual believer.

All of these themes are biblical. Yet all can present difficulties when developed apart from a fuller treatment of the mission of God in the world.

### Christology and the Trinity

The Reformation tradition has clear teaching about the Trinity. But this tradition tends to stress the person and work of Christ in its development of the biblical content. This leads to an emphasis on Christology, an understanding of the person Jesus Christ especially related to the work of salvation. The work of the Father is usually treated in terms of sovereignty and election. The work of the Spirit is usually discussed in terms of the Spirit's saving and sealing work. The treatment of each person of the Trinity tends to make the saving work of Christ the starting point for theology.

A fuller understanding of the work of each of the three persons of the Godhead emerges if we make the mission of God in the world our starting point for understanding their work. God's mission encompasses God's works of creation, re-creation, and consummation, and relates all three persons to all three works. This perspective helps us understand the creation of a church in light of God's being, God's social reality as a Trinity, and the work of all three persons.[2] The ministry of the church, in turn, must reflect all three aspects of the Godhead. In North America today, this calls us to place greater emphasis on the work of the Spirit as the one who creates the church and leads it in ministry.

## The Cross and Creation

The Reformation tradition often treats creation more in terms of a sinless state lost through sin, rather than as a design that points us to the fuller possibilities of redemption. The focus is placed on the cross and the application of its redemptive power to the spiritual life of the believer. Redemption is usually seen as consisting of the work of Christ in forgiving our sins, the Spirit's empowering us for daily living, and God's promise of eternal life. These aspects of redemption are biblical, but do not fully describe the mission of God in the world.

Those who make the cross the starting point for their discussion of redemption often find it difficult to see the bigger picture inherent both in creation design and in God's redemptive reign as announced by Jesus. Starting with an understanding of the mission of God in the world provides a broader framework for considering the meaning of the cross. The cross is still central within this framework, but its purpose is understood in light of the broader scope of God's mission. Understanding the cross in relation to creation is critical to being able to grasp the full character of the church's ministry in the world.

## The Individual and Community

The Reformation tradition also focused on defining the true church and establishing its institutional identity. The Reformers called for a shift away from priests controlling salvation through institutional management of the sacrament of communion. Martin Luther affirmed, instead, the priesthood of all believers. Each person had direct access to God without going through a priest as intermediary. Every individual's worth to God was emphasized. In the midst of later Enlightenment influences, this great truth fed the tendency for salvation to be defined in individualistic terms. Individualistic salvation became common fare in most streams of Protestant theology, but was especially prominent on the United States frontier in the nineteenth century.[3]

Defining salvation in individual terms is biblical, but it is not all that the Bible teaches. The Spirit of God is creating a new community as the body of Christ. While salvation is always individual in its effect, how it is to be offered and experienced is very corporate. To be converted to Christ is to be converted to his body, the church. The church is not a collection of self-selecting individuals who assemble to have their needs met. The church, as the creation of the Spirit, corporately offers salvation to individuals, but this salvation is accepted and experienced within a community.

The ministry of the church grows out of the mission of God in the world. Three aspects of God's mission in the world have direct implications for the ministry of the church: God's cosmic confrontation with the powers, God's reconciling work in the world, and God's redemptive work within the community of faith.

*In your experience what gets the most emphasis?*

The Ministry of the Church

# The Church and the Powers

The Bible presents the story of created life in cosmic terms. Created reality has both natural and supernatural dimensions. In Genesis 1–2, these dimensions worked in harmony within God's creation design, bringing glory to God. Genesis 3 introduces another aspect of this reality, the brokenness that results from disobedience. This disobedience begins with the archangel Satan and those of the heavenly host who joined in the rebellion against God. It is extended to the natural world with the choice by Adam and Eve to eat of the tree of the knowledge of good and evil.

The consequences of this act of disobedience were devastating. All the created powers were broken and at odds with God's created purposes. Everything was out of whack. A new reality existed for Adam and Eve. An alternative force was now at work that could use the fallen powers to challenge God's rightful authority. The Bible presents this force as Satan and his hosts. Satan is presented as the "ruler of the power of the air" (Eph. 2:2), the personal force who exercises control over the created powers that are now fallen and in rebellion against God. These are referred to as the "rulers . . . authorities . . . cosmic powers of this present darkness . . . spiritual forces of evil in the heavenly places" (Eph. 6:10).

In the face of this pervasive evil, the biblical story makes it clear that human beings, as the crown of God's creation, are not without hope. God promised to break the power of the evil one through the "seed of the woman" (Gen. 3:15). This promise introduced grace into the biblical record and is the beginning of the story of redemption. It anticipates the Good News that would one day be announced by Jesus as the inauguration of God's redemptive reign.

The inauguration of God's redemptive reign in Jesus' person and presence was nothing less than this cosmic power encounter. God was breaking into history to directly invade the enemy's territory and defeat Satan's power. The diagram previously introduced in chaper 4 illustrates the point (see fig. 10).

Jesus directly confronted the power of the evil one demonstrating that redemption was now possible in every dimension

**Figure 10**

**The Presence of God's Reign Shaping the Ministry
of the Church**

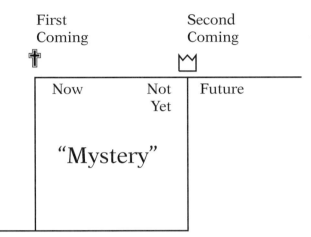

First
Coming

Second
Coming

Now          Not          Future
             Yet

"Mystery"

Present

of life. He taught, for those who had eyes to see and ears to hear, that the new reality of God's redemptive reign was now working within human history. The strong man (Luke 11:21–22) was being bound, and the little flock (Luke 12:32) was being formed as a new type of community. The Spirit would create this community to participate fully in carrying the work of redemption into the world, and he would lead it into a ministry of direct encounter with the fallen powers. An ultimate victory over the forces of evil would one day be realized in a consummation when all sin and the evil one would be judged.

## Creation and Ministry

It is critical to begin our thinking about the ministry of the church with this understanding of the purposes of God in creation, re-creation, and consummation. Unless we do, the church's ministry tends to turn inward, to focus primarily on itself.

The creation sets the parameters for understanding salvation and the work of Christ on the cross. Salvation needs to be

133

understood in relation to the full scope of the created powers within the original creation. The created powers represent the forces of life lodged within the processes and structures of human existence.

It is not just individuals who need salvation. The fall into sin was not just about Adam and Eve's personal guilt before God. It was about the whole of creation rebelling against God. Salvation is about God's bringing back into right relationship all that was lost, apart from Satan and the fallen angels. This bringing back includes the created powers now fallen (Col. 1:15–20).

Unless this more cosmic understanding of creation is kept in view, the scope of salvation is often limited, and the role of the church is often distorted. This can be seen in the relationship of the church to the world in various traditions.[4] Some have viewed the world as a hostile and evil place to be avoided, so that ministry is seen as a work of extracting people from this hostile place to the safety of the church. Some have viewed the world as evil, but a place where individual Christians are to have some influence of moral persuasion, so that ministry involves personally modeling redeemed behavior in the world. Others have worked from the perspective that evil is present in the world, but culture is basically neutral, so that ministry embraces the forms of culture somewhat uncritically, often as tools for enhancing effectiveness.

## Defeating the Powers

None of these perspectives does justice to the plan and purposes of God. God's creation design was cosmic in scope and comprehensive in character. God's re-creation purposes are no less (Eph. 1:9–10). In Colossians Paul points out that God in Christ disarmed the principalities and powers, made a public example of them, and triumphed over them in him (2:15). The created powers, though fallen, are themselves now disarmed. The evil one can no longer use them to control us now that God's redemptive reign has broken in. The fallen world could not stay fallen in Jesus' presence. While the evil one is still present in the world, he does not have ultimate authority.[5]

The Ministry of the Church

## Unmasking the Powers

The defeated powers present the church with a crucial responsibility as it lives its life and carries out its ministry. The church is responsible to unmask the powers that have been disarmed by showing that they no longer have power over the redeemed people of God. As the church lives by the power of the Spirit according to the new nature it has received, it unmasks these once-fallen created powers and demonstrates that they can be redeemed for God's purposes. The challenge before the church is to reclaim lost territory in the whole of creation for the glory and purposes of God. This unmasking is not without pain or conflict since the church is to carry out this ministry in the manner of Jesus as a suffering servant. This unmasking is not without struggle as the church lives between the times of God's redemptive power being present, while the final judgment of evil yet remains.

The unmasking of the powers that have been disarmed means that the church's ministry is a power encounter between God and the forces of evil. This is made plain by Paul in the letter to the Ephesians, where we find that it is "through the church that the manifold wisdom of God is now made known to the principalities and powers in the heavenly places" (3:10). The church's ministry must be framed in cosmic terms. The church's ministry must be framed in power encounter terms. But the church's ministry must also be framed in corporate terms, where the church through the power of the Spirit accepts suffering and pain as part of the privilege of redeemed living. This cosmic framework of understanding the church's ministry places a priority on the relationship of the church to the world. God is not finished with the world in the midst of its sin and brokenness. He wants to bring about reconciliation in all of life.

## The Church's Ministry of Reconciliation

The church's relationship to the world in different periods of history varied depending on the church's self-understanding of its identity and purpose. God intends for the church to define itself over against a fallen world. However, since the Reformation, many churches have tended to define themselves over against other churches based on the two-marks criteria used to test for the true church. As a result, some churches have become inwardly focused, preoccupied with maintaining purity. And many denominations have tended to develop their identities over against one another based on diverse theological views.

These views of the church fail to take seriously the work of God in the world. God is about the mission of reconciliation in the world. Paul states that God has given to the church the "ministry of reconciliation, that is, in Christ God was reconciling the world to himself" (2 Cor. 5:18–19). It is God's purpose to make all things new, reconciling everything to reflect creation intent while looking forward to consummation. For those who are separated from God, this means being brought into right relationship with God and others. These people come into the church, where every aspect of their lives is made new in Christ. As this transformation occurs, they take into the world the fullness of God's power, which overcomes the principalities and powers through transformed living as a new social community.

God has a passion to redeem the whole of creation. He also has a passion for lost people. Both of these passions are conveyed to us through the biblical covenants. Interestingly, teaching on the biblical covenants has often reinforced the church's tendency to minister primarily to its own members. This occurs whenever God's purposes in predestination and election are misconstrued as a form of privilege through the covenants.[6]

God has two purposes in giving covenants. First, God is committed to establishing and strengthening a special relationship with his people. Second, God is committed to working through his people to bring the message of redemption to the rest of the world. God desires to have a special people who will live in right relationship with him and demonstrate to the world the full possibilities of redeemed living. All the biblical covenants bear witness to these purposes. All the biblical covenants are aspects of God's redemptive work in the world which can be summarized as a covenant of redemption, one that complements the covenant of creation (see fig. 11).

The Ministry of the Church

**Figure 11**

**The Biblical Covenants and Redemption**

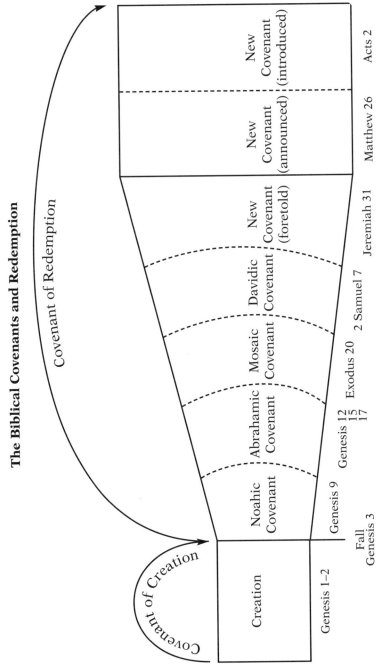

The biblical covenants all carry good news both for the community of God's people and for the rest of the people in the world. These covenants were not intended to grant exclusive privilege to the people of God. God's intent is for this redeemed people to be agents of the ministry of reconciliation being offered to the world.

1. Covenant with Noah. In Genesis 9, God, consistent with creation purposes, affirmed life and promised to protect it by never again sending total destruction and through introducing measures to preserve life.
2. Covenant with Abraham. In Genesis 12, 15, and 17, God revealed a plan to entrust the message of redemption to a special people who would have a special location in the world. Israel's existence in the Promised Land was to function as a blessing or curse to the rest of the nations depending on how they treated God's people. This meant that God's people were to be in relationship with the rest of the nations. God established this covenant by attributing righteousness in response to Abraham's faith.
3. Covenant with Moses. In Exodus 20, God gave the law to Israel. This law came four hundred years after the rite of circumcision had confirmed Israel's covenant relationship with God. The purpose of the Mosaic legislation was to create a holy nation. The sanctified living of Israel as a people before the nations was to serve as a city on the hill and a light to the Gentiles to draw them to faith in the living God.
4. Covenant with David. In 2 Samuel 7, God promised the coming of a son who would be a king. The people of God had an earthly king who served on behalf of God, but God was to be the true king. God promised that his own son would be the king of this people and that the son's throne would reign forever. This reign would redemptively relate the people of God to the rest of the world.
5. New Covenant Foretold. In Jeremiah 31, God promised a new covenant. God knew that Israel was continuing to live in disobedience, so God promised to give them the

power necessary to live out the reality of redemption in the world. This power was the promised indwelling of the Spirit who would help the people of God live as the new humanity. As a new community, they would be responsible to invite all humanity into a right relationship with God.

6. New Covenant Anticipated. In Matthew 26, Jesus made clear that his life ministry was the establishment of the new covenant and that this new covenant was founded on the redemption accomplished through the shedding of his blood. This would open to all peoples direct access to the grace of God and participation in the new community created by the Spirit.

7. New Covenant Introduced. In Acts 2, the new covenant was fulfilled in the work of the Spirit at Pentecost, creating a new community from among people of all the nations of the world. This new community, the church, was expected to carry God's message and invitation to the ends of the earth.

This covenantal understanding of the ministry of reconciliation means that the church does not exist only for itself. It belongs to God and is to involve itself fully in the redemptive work of God in the world. Placing these themes together—covenant and kingdom—provides perspective on the fuller purposes of the Triune God in all of creation. It is this framework which provides the foundation for thinking in terms of a missiological ecclesiology. In such a view, the mission of God is inseparably woven into our view of the church (see fig. 12).

The church lives within God's redemptive reign. The church lives between the times of the introduction of the blessing of the Spirit and the final judgement of sin. In this position, the church is a clear demonstration to the world that heaven has already begun. From this position, God uses the church as a sign, foretaste, and instrument to invite all humanity and all creation to come to know fully the living and true God.

139

# Figure 12

## God's Covenant-Kingdom Plan and the Ministry of the Church

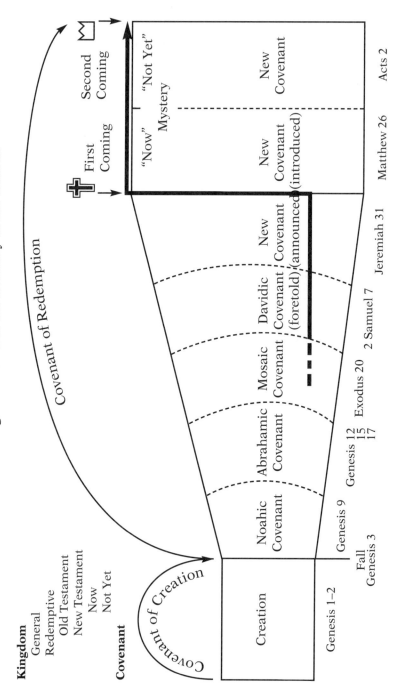

# The Dynamics of the Church's Ministry

Stan worked at the nearby state university as a staff member for Campus Crusade for Christ. This particular Sunday morning he was speaking in an adult education forum at Calvin Presbyterian Church. Several students involved in his ministry on campus attended here, and they had persuaded the pastor to invite Stan to talk about his ministry.

Stan had laid out the biblical theme from Matthew 28 of making disciples of all nations and had stressed the importance of getting new converts into Bible study and encouraging them to share their faith with others. "This is essential to the process of developing mature believers," he said.

At this point, Mr. Bradford, a longtime church elder, asked, "How do you see the local church fitting into this process? In particular, how do you see preaching and sacraments as marks of the true church relating to what you do?"

Stan was not prepared for this question. He had heard the language of "marks" once in another conversation, but wasn't sure what this meant. He paused for a moment, then responded, "Well, we encourage all our students to be actively involved in a local church in addition to being part of our fellowship on campus. But we stay away from taking any positions on the sacraments. Not only does it seem to cause controversy, but we think it's more important to get people into personal Bible study and prayer."

Mr. Bradford quietly responded, "Aren't you really a church, even though you don't call yourself one?"

Stan sensed he was in over his head at this point and asked if there were any other questions.

Historical ecclesiologies like that held by Mr. Bradford often clash with more functional views like the one held by Stan. What norms does the Bible provide for shaping the church's ministry?

As we consider the ministry of the church, it is essential to keep in mind the church's dual nature as both spiritual and human.[7] This means the church will operate by different dynamics from what the world perceives as natural. These

141

dynamics involve the Bible in relation to the Spirit, the reality of grace, and the gifts of the Spirit.

## Marks of the Church: Led and Taught by the Spirit

When the Reformers sought to establish specific marks that could distinguish a true church from a false church, they were not operating in a vacuum. They were addressing perceived abuses in the Roman Catholic Church. Most importantly, they sought to recover biblical preaching, to once again make the Word of God central to the life of congregations. They also sought to restore the sacraments as a means of grace for believers in place of their being used to establish or maintain salvation.

The selection of these Reformation marks was context-shaped. They reflect the emphases needed to correct specific perceived abuses in the Roman Catholic Church in the sixteenth century. While these marks were intended to speak to the distinguishing characteristics of the true church in general, they apply most directly to local congregations. Here the marks become specific ministry functions that congregations are responsible to carry out. But rather than defining ministry in terms of a specific historical context and local congregations, it is more useful to develop an understanding of the church's ministry in light of the biblical teaching on God's redemptive purposes. This approach leads us to focus on the work of the Spirit.

A biblical emphasis on the Spirit's work in the church stresses two activities—leading and teaching. The Spirit leads the church into the powerful presence of God's redemptive reign, and the Spirit teaches the church on how to live within this reign. Instead of preaching and sacraments, the marks of the church might better be framed as "led by the Spirit" and "taught by the Spirit," or more accurately, "governed by the Word as it is led and taught by the Spirit."

Jesus promised that he would not leave his followers alone. He was going to send them an Advocate-Helper who would lead them in carrying out their ministry and teach them what they

142

needed to know. Jesus tied the Spirit's leading and teaching to both the Scriptures of the Old Testament ("he opened their minds to understand the scriptures" [Luke 24:45]), and the instruction Jesus had given ("the Advocate . . .[will] remind you of all that I have said to you" [John 14:26]). This relationship between the Spirit and the revealed Word of God extended to new revelation: "Say whatever is given you at that time, for it is not you who speak, but the Holy Spirit" (Mark 13:11). How do these marks of the Spirit's leading and teaching the church function for us today?

## Led by the Spirit: Corporate Life

An important Protestant confession, the Belgic Confession, was formulated in 1566 for the Reformed churches of the Southern Netherlands.[8] Of the Reformation confessions, it came closest to identifying the purpose of the marks criteria. Article 29, The Marks of the True Church, says that the true church "engages in the pure preaching of the gospel; it makes use of the pure administration of the sacraments as Christ instituted them; it practices church discipline for correcting faults." This is followed by a summary statement: "In short, [the true church] governs itself according to the pure Word of God. . . ." This statement expresses the larger intent of the more specific marks.

The church's life is to be governed by the Word. While the confession statement says that the church "governs itself," it might more aptly be stated that "the church is governed in all its life by the Word." An even more biblically correct formulation might be, "the church governs all its life by the Word as it is led and taught by the Spirit."

The Reformers' intent was to return the Word to the center of life within local congregations. But singling out preaching and sacraments can produce several problems in how the ministry of the church is understood and practiced. These include (a) the tendency to limit the primary communication of the Word to the activity of preaching; (b) the tendency to see only ordained persons as qualified to minister through communicating the Word of God and dispensing the sacraments; and (c) limiting the focus of worship to the act of preaching.

Being governed by the Word means that the church's life and ministry are to be defined by the biblical story. The church must live into this story, seeking to understand the full purposes of God. The church must also live out of this story, applying God's purposes to its life and ministry.

As the church lives "into" and "out of" the biblical story, its life is transformed by its power. The biblical story is contextualized in the life of the church. The church becomes, in fact, the hermeneutic of the gospel. That is, the world is able to understand the truthfulness of the gospel story by reading the story of the life of the church.

For the full intent of God's story to be understood and applied in a specific context, the church must approach the Bible as a whole. Many churches make selective use of certain passages, themes, and/or verses. These churches often end up living out a reductionistic version of the gospel for the world to read. Many churches have also adopted cultural practices without critiquing them in light of the full power of the biblical narrative. These churches often become captive to a secular worldview. To avoid these problems, the church must start with the bigger picture of God's creation design and redemptive purposes.

## Taught by the Spirit: Corporate Faith

Understanding the Bible's message is not just a process of using human reason to discern biblical truths. The process is supernatural: "these things God has revealed to us through the Spirit" (1 Cor. 2:10). The Spirit uses the Bible to guide the church into all truth. Paul mentioned this connection when he committed the Ephesian elders to the leading of God's Spirit and the ministry of God's Word in their midst (Acts 20:28, 32). Paul was saying that a congregation within the apostolic tradition that has the Word of God and the Spirit of God has sufficient resources to guide it in carrying out its ministry.

The Ministry of the Church

Understanding the Bible is not a matter of private judgment. Biblical truth is corporate truth. As believers study the Bible, it is important that they draw on historical understandings of the biblical story and engage in interpreting the Bible as a corporate faith community, with an interpretation consistent with the apostolic tradition. These conditions for understanding and interpreting the Bible introduce several critical points.

First, we need to understand how the Spirit's teaching helps the church formulate confessions and make policy choices. Confessions need to be valued and used to enhance the church's understanding of the Bible. Confessions are not Scripture, but they can serve as important guides in helping the church understand Scripture and apply it in making policy decisions. Because confessions are time-bound, they need to be understood in relation to the dynamic ministry of the Spirit.[9] The Spirit continues to lead the church into all truth, especially in relationship to the specific contexts in which the church lives.

Second, we need to understand that the biblical story is inherently translatable.[10] God's eternal truths came to the church clothed in human cultures. These truths, in turn, can be understood and applied in different contexts. In confessing the truth and making policy decisions, the church should always be a little humble regarding any claims of an absolute understanding of truth. All understandings of the Word function as an interpretation of absolute truth within a given context. These interpretations are authoritative because they represent the authority of God's Word, but they are nevertheless always conditioned to some extent by their context.

Third, we need to place a high value on the diversity of gifts the Spirit gives the church for carrying out ministry. Many of these gifts are directly linked to understanding and communicating the Bible within the community of faith. No one gift has the primary privilege of presenting God's truth. The Spirit uses a variety of speaking gifts for this purpose: prophecy, teaching, exhorting, knowledge, wisdom, and pastor-teacher. Our understanding of the Word is enhanced when we get different perspectives on the Word through the variety of the gifts given by the Spirit.

# Grace-Based and Gift-Shaped Ministry

The Spirit is the source of the church's life and power. This life and power operate in the church in two distinct ways. The Spirit administers the grace of God within the community, resulting in grace-based ministry. And the Spirit empowers believers within the community to function as channels of grace to one another, resulting in gift-shaped ministry.

## Grace-Based Church Life and Ministry

Believers are justified and incorporated into the church by grace through faith: "For by grace you have been saved through faith. . . ." (Eph. 2:8–9). The sanctification of believers and their spiritual formation within community is also by grace through faith: "He who raised Christ from the dead will give life to your mortal bodies also through his Spirit that dwells in you" (Rom. 8:11). To say that church life is grace-based means that it is the result of God's working for us and within us. Grace is God's divine favor given without condition to those who are without merit. We can do nothing to earn our salvation, either our justification or sanctification. What we can and must do is respond to the work of the Spirit out of grateful obedience to what God has done and desires to do on behalf of the church.

There is a discipline to grace-based living. Living by grace requires the church to make intentional choices to obey God and act on God's promises. To say ministry is grace-based means that the Spirit is working in and through the church to carry out God's redemptive purposes. Because the church is a social reality, the grace of God is a social reality. This means that grace operates within a communal framework. The work of the Spirit is to apply grace within the community and to empower the community by grace to implement ministry. One key to understanding this ministry is the relationship between grace and giftedness.

## Gift-Shaped Church Life and Ministry

God's intent is to establish the church as a new humanity in the midst of fallen humanity, as a demonstration of the fullness of redemptive possibilities. All human behaviors are capable of being transformed by grace. They can be redeemed for God's purposes. This redemption is accomplished in part through the spiritual gifts God has given to the church.

Ephesians 4 provides a powerful picture of the church living as a grace-based, gift-shaped community. Christ gives spiritual gifts to each member of the community (7). While some with leadership gifts are themselves gifts to the church, their role is to help develop the gifts of all the members, "to equip the saints for the work of ministry, for building up the body of Christ until all of us come to . . . unity . . . knowledge . . . maturity" (12–13). These gifts help the church live redemptively in a broken world: "We must no longer be children, tossed to and fro and blown about" (14). They promote the growth of the church in every dimension when each part is working (16). Grace flows into the body, through the body, and to each member within the body through the exercise of these gifts.

This is why we are called "members one of another" (Rom. 12:5–6). Our lives in the church community are woven into a common social fabric, forming a redeemed community that is to live as a new humanity. This can only take place as the Spirit empowers each person for sanctified living, which in turn can only take place as the Spirit's gifts given to each person become channels of grace operating within and through the church.

The corporate nature of the church is foundational for understanding its ministry. It means that we must start with corporate spiritual formation before proceeding to the spiritual formation of individual members.

*Eph 4*

*class: what do you think of this?*

147

# The Church's Practice of Ministry

To be true to its nature, the church's practice of ministry must contribute to the formation and building of community. As we have seen, the primary biblical images of church all relate to its being a social community. This community is presented as (a) a people of God who live by a different power and a different politic in the world; (b) the body of Christ whose members live in a complementary relationship with one another; (c) the communion of saints living as a new type of humanity in community; and (d) a creation of the Spirit to which people continue to be added.

*review of primary images*

The church as a social community is under the supervision of the Spirit. But the Spirit works through leaders who are qualified, gifted, selected, and confirmed within the church. This leadership, in concert with the leading, teaching, and empowerment of the Spirit, are responsible for carrying out the practices of ministry. This ministry takes place primarily, though not exclusively, in communities of faith we know as local congregations.

## The Sacraments and Ministry

Since the church is by nature a community, for the church's ministry to be true to its nature, all its ministry practices must be shaped by this reality. For example, the sacraments of baptism and the Lord's Supper are not merely personal means of grace; their greater purpose is to build and nurture the life of the community. The Bible makes it clear that baptism is to be the distinct point of entry into a congregation. The Bible also makes it clear that a congregation, as a community of God's people, is to celebrate the Lord's Supper at the center of its communal living.

### Baptism: Entrance into the Community

Baptism is a missional act proclaiming to the world that God is calling, shaping, and sending a people for mission. By baptism, new initiates are welcomed as full participants into a covenantal community. This act of initiation symbolizes that the old way of living is "dead" and that a new nature is now

148

"alive through the power of the Spirit" (Romans 6). Because the church is a social reality with a spiritual nature, persons can only become part of the church if they share the new nature that comes from the Spirit.

Baptism represents a public, corporate statement to both the church and the world that the initiate is now made new and is joining a community of faith that is being led and taught by the Spirit. It is obvious that there are two theological traditions within the church regarding baptism. One applies baptism to believers and their children, while the other applies it only to those making profession. In both traditions, the basic point remains the same. Baptism functions as the act of entrance into the community, whether by a promise that must later be personally owned by the recipient, or by profession of personal faith.

### The Lord's Supper: Celebrating Life in Community

Celebrating the Lord's Supper nurtures the life of the church community. First, it serves as a means for experiencing the riches of the grace of God. Therefore, the church is to confess its sins. Second, it serves as a reminder that Christ's body was broken and his blood was shed for all. Therefore, the church is to share freely this message with others. Third, it reminds the church and the world that there is an answer to the world's spiritual hungers. Therefore, the church is joyfully to share the Good News. Fourth, it reminds the church and the world that there is an answer to the world's physical hungers. Therefore, the church is freely to share its own bread with those in physical need.

The sacraments establish boundaries and provide spiritual nourishment for the church. But the ministry of the church is more than just hearing the Word and celebrating the sacraments.

## Core Biblical Ministry Functions

Because the church is a community, its ministry is to be not only grace-based and gift-shaped but also community-centered. The Bible describes certain core ministry functions that are essential to the shared life and work of the community.

One of the most comprehensive biblical passages that outlines these ministry functions is Paul's teaching on the church

**Figure 13**

**Core Functions of Church Life in Romans 12**

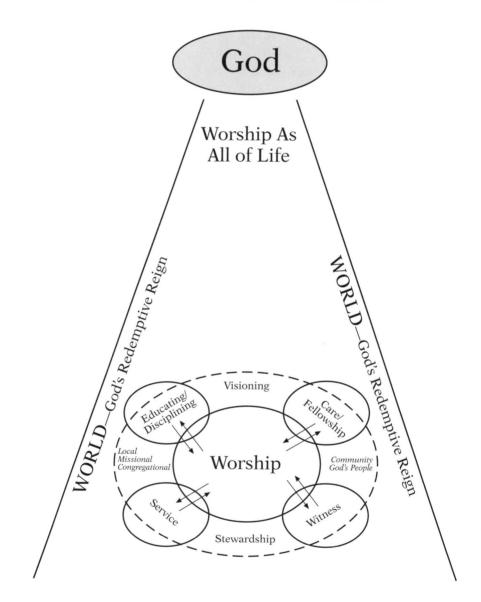

in Romans 12. This chapter provides a framework for understanding the different dimensions of life and ministry in local congregations. Here Paul defines the core biblical functions that shape the life of the church as a community (see fig. 13).

### All of Life As Worship

Paul introduces his teaching about church life by stressing that the church is a social community with spiritual empowerment. Paul addresses the recipients of this teaching in the plural, meaning that he is speaking to the church as a community. He draws on the Old Testament image of sacrifice, calling on the church to be a living sacrifice that is holy and acceptable (see Exodus 12, Passover Lamb; and Leviticus 16, Day of Atonement). Paul calls this our "spiritual worship" or "reasonable service." The term used here for worship or service is used in the New Testament to represent the sacrificial system of the Mosaic law with all its accompanying prescriptions for righteous living.[11] Paul is saying to the church of the new covenant that intentionally living in a relational community in right relationship both with God and with one another is equivalent to obeying the rigorous details of the Old Testament law. This spiritual worship characterizes all of life. It is the lifestyle of the community as a whole, and it finds expression in a variety of ministry practices.

### Specific Worship

Specific worship takes place as the community gathers to praise God, give glory to God, and listen to God. Such worship serves a centering function in the life of the church. The spiritual empowerment received in worship flows into the other dimensions of ministry. In turn, the energy and fruit of the other ministry practices flow into the corporate worship. Congregations that cultivate the practice of joyful, devoted worship gain perspective and power for living all of life as worship.

The elements of worship include praise, singing, prayer, hearing the Word, giving, and preparing for service in the world. The specifics of how these are shaped in terms of order, style, and format are left to the responsible decision-making of the church under the leading and teaching of the Spirit. Consistent with the nature of the church as universal and local, ministry practices reflect contextual characteristics. Also consistent with the nature of the church being one and many, ministry practices seek to reflect sound historical teaching established within the larger church.

## Discipling

Every believer is to grow into full maturity in Christ. Discipleship, though intensely personal, is corporate in character (12:3–5). We see this in two ways. First, spiritual maturity involves growth in the fruit of the Spirit. Spiritual fruit assumes the engagement of social relationships and can only be developed in relationship to other persons. The Christian community offers the best environment for the nurture of the fruit of the Spirit.

Second, the corporate character of discipleship is seen in the development of spiritual gifts (12:6–8). The gifts of the Spirit are given to each member of the body to be used in community to benefit others. In turn, being in community opens up each believer to the gift-shaped ministry of others. As grace flows through gift-shaped ministry, each believer becomes more mature in obeying all the biblical mandates, even in those areas where they are not gifted. For example, being around someone with the gift of serving enhances one's capacity to serve. Grace flows through gifts and nurtures the formation of spiritual fruit.

## Fellowshiping

God's grace flows through the body in fellowship. The church's nature as a social community makes it self-evident that fellowshiping is to be a ministry practice of the church. In sharing Christ in common, Christians are called to live as fully reconciled to both God and one another. Fellowship, in this sense, is living out behaviors that characterize what it means to come together in community (12:9–12). Paul is making the point that the cultivation of such Christian behavior is tied to being in relationship with others. Fellowship with other believers is necessary for developing personal spiritual growth.

doesn't support his point

What other passages point to discipleship

When believers are in community, a demonstration of spiritual power occurs. When "two or three" are gathered together in Jesus' name (Matt. 18:20), it is not just a social gathering. God is present. The Spirit is at work strengthening, convicting, healing, shaping, and encouraging persons as they relate in community. God's power is made evident as the community demonstrates a new type of humanity on earth. Spirit-empowered fellowship has a big impact on those who come into contact with Christian community. This was perhaps the primary way in which the church in Jerusalem grew. Fellowship is itself a powerful witness.

## Serving

The church is to demonstrate a new lifestyle before the world, one that breaks the cycle of anger, reaction, and revenge that characterizes the world's practices. The core of this lifestyle is to be Christian service. Christians are to serve both fellow believers and unbelievers, even when they are hostile and mistreat us (12:14–21).

makes me think of Volf Exclusion and Embrace

This ministry of service becomes an act of witness, a demonstration of grace that unmasks the powers. The world, in not being able to provoke the church into hostile reaction, discovers its own bondage. The Bible assumes that living in service to one another and toward the world will be more than just individual actions; it will involve the corporate actions of communities. There is grace-filled power in the church's communal acts of service.

## Witness

Just as service is a corporate responsibility of the church, so also is witness (12:14–27). As the church lives before the world as a new humanity, there will be opportunities to give a word of witness that explains the "hope that is in you" (1 Peter 3:15). Witness is not about program and method. It is about openly inviting others into the community of new humanity so they can experience the grace of God.

Congregations that are dynamically experiencing the grace and power of being a new community have little difficulty offering this invitation. Those who come into contact with such churches are often open to such an invitation. The grace of God flows to lost persons through the words of witness coming from communities that are experiencing the transforming power of the Spirit.

### Visioning

The church is called to represent the redemptive power of God on earth. Congregations are responsible to discern how the power of God's reign can best relate to the specifics of their contexts. This discernment process is called visioning, or the development of visionary faith. Visionary faith brings into focus a contextual and redemptive answer to the prayer, "Your kingdom come, your will be done, on earth as it is in heaven" (Matt. 6:10). Congregations need visionary faith to shape the direction of their ministry and guide the choices necessary for carrying it out. Visioning together fosters a common bond among the members of the community as a distinct people of God in their place.

### Stewarding

Stewardship of the resources God has provided is a critical ministry function. This responsibility is inherent in the ministry of the church both in terms of creation design and re-creation intent. If God is going to demonstrate to the world that all things can be brought back to right relationship, then the church's practice of stewardship is an important demonstration of such possibilities.

Stewardship includes not only a wise use of resources, but also compassionate care for the needs of all the members. God's grace flows through the body as resources are shared. God's grace is demonstrated to the world as the church shows how all of life can be brought under stewardship for redemptive living.

All these aspects of the church's ministry are rooted in the church's nature. Just as the nature of the church is to shape its ministry practices, the nature and ministry of the church must determine its organizational life. That is the topic of chapter 7.

The Ministry of the Church

# The Organizational Life of the Church

"It's so complex," thought Sarah as she sat through another board meeting of the Springdale Community Services Agency (SCSA). This agency was formed ten years earlier to coordinate community efforts in addressing human service issues. The board was getting ready for its annual fund-raising drive. They had just decided to visit all twenty-six churches in the community to strengthen community networking and fund-raising efforts by the agency.

Sarah was a little skeptical of this strategy. "Why do there have to be so many different Christian churches and organizations," she wondered, "with all of them seeming to be so protective of their own turf?" As she accepted her assignment of making four visits with Charles, she commented, "I sure hope that at least some of these churches have a vision for something bigger than their own survival and growth."

A complex variety of organizational structures: that is how we encounter the church in North America. How are we to think about these various forms? What purposes do they serve? What validity do they have? How are we to understand their existence?

This book discusses the relationship between the nature, ministry, and organization of the church. What is critical is to establish and maintain this relationship in the right sequence. The nature of the church provides the basis for understanding the ministry of the church—the church is. The ministry of the church provides the framework for under-

155

standing the organization of the church—the church does what it is. The organization of the church provides the structures for the church to carry out its ministry—the church organizes what it does.

In thinking about how the church uses structures to support ministry, it is helpful to remind ourselves of the key elements of the church's ministry that have a direct bearing on its organization.

> The ministry of the church is a power encounter between God and the evil one.
>
> The ministry of the church is based on God's disarming the powers through Christ.
>
> The ministry of the church is about unmasking the powers that have been disarmed.
>
> The church's ministry is to bring God's redemptive reign to all of life.
>
> The church's ministry is to be governed by the Word as it is led and taught by the Spirit.
>
> The church's ministry is to be grace-based and gift-shaped.

This chapter explores the work of the Spirit guiding the continual development of the organizational life of the visible church. First, a number of preliminary issues that affect this process are discussed. Then the two primary structures that emerged in the organizational life of the church in the first century are presented, along with the connectional processes that were used to maintain unity and a common faith. This is followed by review of the types of leaders and the role of leadership as it developed within the church.

This presentation represents a basic biblical framework for thinking about the organization of the church. Applying this framework to the historical development of the church and to the church as it now exists in North America is an important next step which exceeds the purpose of this book.[1] (This chapter focuses how the church in the first century came to organize the ministry of the church in that context.)

# The Church Organizes What It Does

Organization is essential to the church's existence. Organizational structures are inherent within the nature of the church as catholic and contextual in the world. Organization expresses the church's ministry in concrete ways. It is the most visible dimension of the church's life. It is also one of the most powerful aspects for shaping the lives and behaviors of those who participate in the church.

Organization binds people together through shared structures, connectional processes, and leadership roles. The church shapes structures to implement its ministry, develops connectional processes to govern its life, and selects leaders to help guide these activities. While the church shares these features—structure, processes, and leadership—in common with other organizations, because the church is more than a human enterprise, these matters cannot be treated exclusively from a human perspective.

Organizational dimensions of church life, though influenced by cultural patterns and historical circumstances, are not arbitrary. Their shape is influenced by the work of the Spirit in creating, leading, and teaching the church. This began with its development during the New Testament period and has continued throughout history. In reflecting on the development of organization, it is important to note some of its primary functions and to address some of its influences in defining the identity of the church in the world.

## An Institutional Identity for the Church

In dealing with matters of church structure, processes, and leadership, the key is to start by considering the nature of the church, proceed to understanding the ministry of the church, and then move to the development of organization in the church. This relationship and sequence is not always easy to maintain. As the church was created by the Spirit, it quickly began to develop an organizational life. By the end of the first century, this organizational life was taking on institutional characteristics.

On the one hand, the visible church's taking on an institutional identity is a natural development, one the Bible anticipates and legitimizes. The church had to organize itself to represent God's authority in the world. This authority came to be lodged in structures, processes, and leadership roles.

On the other hand, the Bible also makes it clear that the emerging historical, institutional church was never intended to be an end in itself. While the church must have organization, its organizational life must be consistent with the nature of the church and function in support of its ministry. It is critical that the institutional church continue to flow from, find its rationale within, and be maintained consistent with the nature and ministry of the church.

## Institutionalization

The reality of the institutional church needs to be distinguished from the dynamics of institutionalization. Institutionalization is the process whereby particular organizational characteristics become legitimized as official forms and normative practices.[2] Once this legitimization takes place, it is often difficult to introduce change. It becomes all too easy for the medium to distort or displace the message. Organization within the church was never intended to displace the inner dynamic of the nature of the church, or the functional responsibilities of the ministry of the church. The rightful role of organization within the visible church has always been to serve the purposes of the nature and ministry of the church under the continued creating, leading, and teaching of the Spirit.

As noted in chapter 2, a missiological ecclesiology must be developed from four sources: (a) biblical foundations, (b) historical developments, (c) contextual conditions, and (d) the ongoing developmental work of the Spirit. The church is not static; it is a living, dynamic social and spiritual reality. This means that the organizational life of the church must be able to respond to growth, development, and change.

The Organizational Life of the Church

## Growth, Development, and Change

It is important for the church to recognize the limits of particular organizational forms which become institutionalized. All aspects of the church's organizational life—its structures, processes, and leadership roles—are contextual and missionary. They reflect the nature of the church as both catholic and apostolic. While the purposes they serve are unchanging, the particular forms developed to carry out these purposes are not absolute, neither are they static and unchanging. The church's organizational life should be expected to go through growth, development, and change. New forms will emerge as new contexts are encountered, and existing forms will be adapted as circumstances change.

What is crucial in this process is for the church to maintain a balance among biblical foundations, historical developments, and contextual realities. Some tend to absolutize biblical forms as if God ordained a specific organizational pattern for the church to follow, and so they seek to replicate the biblical pattern for the church's structure, processes, and leadership. Some tend to make certain historical forms into a normative polity for the church in all times and all places.[4] These approaches are common in churches stemming from the Protestant Reformation where ecclesiology and polity focused on identifying and maintaining the true, institutional church. Some tend to make the church fit new cultural contexts with little regard for biblical principles and historical developments.[5] They use a pragmatic decision-making approach on the premise that what works is of the Spirit and must, therefore, be biblical. All three approaches plague the church today. All three remind us how important it is for the church to be flexible and adaptive within new contexts and changing circumstances, which is what we find in the New Testament church.

## Development and Variety in the New Testament Church

The church's responsibility to be both redemptive and relevant in its organizational life is clearly evident in the New Testament. Here we find a church that created a variety of forms and practices as it emerged within different contexts. This process is consistent with the nature of the church being catholic and contextual. Some have suggested that there is a development within the church practices of leadership and office in the various epistles usually assigned to Paul.[6] Others suggest that the variety found in the church practices of leadership and office is more a function of the church adapting to different contexts.[7] Regardless of the perspective taken, the basic point is the same. The church in the New Testament was dynamic and diverse in relation to its organizational forms.

In the early writings such as the Thessalonian and Corinthian letters, we find a church trying to apply an understanding of God's redemptive reign to various social and cultural issues such as sexuality, marriage, meat offered to idols, and worship procedures. Ministry is viewed as primarily charismatic and functional, and all members are to participate.

In the more general writings such as Ephesians and Colossians, we find a church seeking to apply an understanding of God's redemptive reign to a broader theological framework of creation-redemption. Ministry is viewed as being both charismatic and role-based, where some persons are themselves gifts to the church for the equipping of all the members for ministry. In the Titus and Timothy letters, we find a church that has existed for some time. The emphasis is on affirming positive behaviors and correcting errant practices. Ministry is viewed as primarily role-defined, being established in the church through specific offices.

Just as the Spirit led the church in developing structures, processes, and leadership roles to fit the various contexts it encountered, we should expect the Spirit to continue to lead the church in developing organizational forms appropriate to a variety of contexts. It is our task to take the whole of the biblical teaching and continue to examine the principles and practices that are instructive for the church as it encounters new contexts in today's world. This should be done while reflecting carefully on how the church throughout its history has applied these principles and practices to diverse contexts.

## Organization As Witness

Because the church is a social community that is both holy and human, everything the church does in the world is to bear witness to the purposes of God and his redemptive power. Church organization—how the church develops its structures, processes, and leadership roles—is itself a form of witness to the world. It witnesses to the fact that here exists a social community that possesses a spiritual character. It is a witness that a redemptive use of power is possible within a human community. This witness can be either positive or negative depending on how faithfully the organization of the church expresses its nature and ministry.

This means that church polity—how the church organizes itself—is of crucial importance for the visible church's full participation in the redemptive reign of God. First of all, church polity must never become an end in itself. The church's organizational practices must be maintained as servant tools to shape the church's ministry as it fully lives out its nature. Second of all, church polity must always be seen as contextual and provisional. Maintaining these perspectives is crucial for keeping a proper perspective on the relationship between organization and power.

## Organization and Power

God's authority is represented on earth through the church. This authority finds expression through becoming structured within the organizational life and practices of the church. Offices, agencies, boards, policies, confessions, and programs are all vehicles for expressing the nature and ministry of the church, but they are neither neutral nor values-free. All express some aspect of power as they relate to the exercise of God's authority within the church. While they share common characteristics with the forms of other organizations, in the church they are intended to express the redemptive purposes of God.

God's redemptive purposes take place within an arena of a power encounter. This occurs between the church and the fallen principalities and powers as the church is led by the Spirit in the world. In this power encounter, the church is to live by a different set of values and exhibit a different set of behaviors. An example of this occurs when Jesus teaches his disciples about leadership (Matt. 20:24–28). Clearly, there would be leaders in the anticipated church, but these leaders were not to function like the Gentiles who lorded it over their followers. A church leader was to function as a servant to those being led. This alerts the church to the danger that the fallen powers can masquerade under the guise of spiritual language in organizational forms in the church.

In being led and taught by the Spirit, the church must maintain a constant vigil to insure that its practices are, in fact, leading to the unmasking of the principalities and powers in the world. It must work to discern and change those practices that become tied to the powers that need to be unmasked. This is a difficult vigil to maintain, especially once particular practices become part of a church's tradition and identity. What functioned as a redemptive servant in one generation can all too easily become a coercive master in the next, as observed in the controversy often associated with making even simple changes in an order of worship.[8]

## Biblical Foundations for Understanding Church Organization

Paul was an active member of Springdale United Church of Christ and contributed generously to the church's budget. But Paul's passion was youth ministry and his church just didn't seem to know what to do when it came to youth. After trying to work in this ministry area in his church for several years, Paul's frustration caught up with him, and he became a volunteer working with Young Life at the Springdale High School.

Being involved in this work was great. The ministry was growing rapidly, and scores of youth were making professions of faith. Paul worked primarily with the small group discipling process. But after a while, the same old issue came back. "How are we supposed to relate what we're doing in Young Life to the churches in Springdale?" Paul didn't have an answer, but he kept thinking there had to be a place for both types of ministry. He thought, "I wonder if the Bible has anything to say about this?"

The New Testament is the starting point for thinking about the organizational life of the church. It describes a rich variety of organizational expressions. The church developed as it expanded into various contexts, which gives us an important clue to its organization. Organization needs to be understood as normative in relation to the purposes it serves, but primarily functional in relation to the particular cultural forms utilized. Particular forms will tend to vary from context to context in accomplishing the same redemptive purpose. This has not always been an easy perspective for the church to maintain.

## Organization in the New Testament Church

The early church selected the word *ecclesia* as its preferred self-designation. As noted earlier, this word came out of secular usage where it referred to an official political assembly being called into session. The church's use of this term to define itself indicates that it viewed its existence as an alternative politic to the human governments of that day. The New Testament uses this term in three different ways.

### A Local Congregation

First, *ecclesia* (church) was used to describe those who gathered together as believers in local congregations. It was common to identify such congregations by their geographic location, such as "the church of God that is in Corinth" (1 Cor. 1:2). It was also common to identify such congregations with those who either hosted or led them in their homes, as in the book of Romans, "Greet Prisca and Aquila . . . also the church in their house" (16:3, 5). In time, scores of such local congregations of the church were scattered across the Mediterranean world, all referred to as churches. A congregation is an *ecclesia*, a called out assembly for the purpose of being the people of God in a particular place.

### A Regional Cluster

Second, *ecclesia* was used in both the singular and plural to identify believers who lived in a general region. An example of this can be found in Acts: "Meanwhile, the church throughout Judea, Galilee, and Samaria had peace and was built up" (9:31). This usage can also be found in Paul's letters: "We want you to know . . . about the grace of God that has been granted to the churches of Macedonia" (2 Cor. 8:1). These uses of the term show that the emerging community of faith thought of the church as more than just a congregation. They thought of the church being congregations, and these congregations had a collective existence that could be designated by the term *ecclesia*.

### The Whole Church

Third, *ecclesia* was used both in the singular and plural to refer to all who belonged to Christ, regardless of where they lived in the world. What later became expressed as the "one" and "catholic" attributes of the church can be found in Ephesians where Paul discusses the church's participation in the power encounter with the forces of evil: "so that through the church the wisdom of God in its rich variety might now be made known to the rulers and authorities in the heavenly places" (3:10). This usage can be found in the plural in Paul's letter to the Romans: "All the churches of Christ greet you" (16:16).

These three uses of the *ecclesia* are instructive for understanding the organizational life of the church. There are local congregations. There are regional clusters of such congregations that sometimes take collective action. There is the visible church throughout the world whose presence bears witness to the redemptive reign of God. These expressions of the church are to relate in fellowship, engage in cooperative actions, and make collective choices regarding the ministry of the church.

In developing an ecclesiology and shaping an organizational polity, all three aspects of fellowship, actions, and choices need to be taken into account. Integration of life, cooperation in actions, and the making of collective decisions should be reflected in the church's organizational life.

The Organizational Life of the Church

## Local and Mobile Structures, and Connectional Processes

The visible church in all its diversity is to maintain integration, develop cooperation, and support collective action as it engages in missionizing local contexts and the broader world. To accomplish this, the developing New Testament church operated out of two distinct structures—local missional congregations and mobile missional structures. These structures related to each other through a series of connectional processes (see fig. 14).

**Figure 14**

**Local and Mobile Structures and Connectional Processes in the Visible Church**

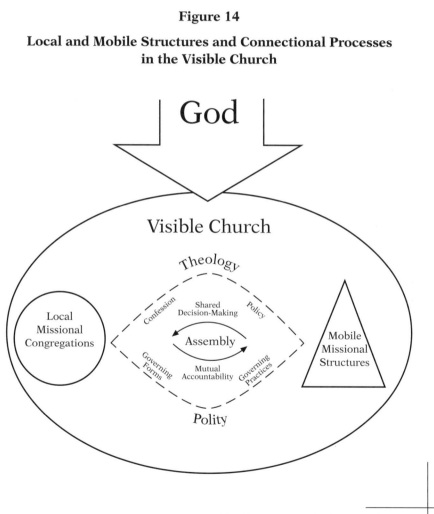

The Organizational Life of the Church

### Local Missional Congregations

Local missional congregations are a primary organizational structure of church life. This is evident in the development of church life in the first century as local, regional, and global. It is also implicit in all the core biblical images for the church— people of God, body of Christ, communion of saints, and creation of the Spirit. These images, all focusing on the church as a social community, imply that concrete communities of reconciled people will exist in the world. Such communities, of necessity, will be located within local contexts and reflect the characteristics of specific times and places.

Local congregations are the primary and most assessable structure of the organizational development of the visible church. As discussed in the last chapter, the ministry of the local church involves a variety of functions (see fig. 15).

Because the church is catholic and local, the creating work of the Spirit means that congregations will be contextual, and therefore diverse. Reflecting such diversity and contextuality, the New Testament exhibits a variety of types of local congregations. No one model of a New Testament local congregation can be found.

1. *Temple congregation and house fellowships.* In Acts 2–6, the early Christians gathered regularly at the temple to hear the teaching of the apostles, where they commingled their Jewish heritage with their newfound Christian faith. Dynamically related to this temple worship was the practice of these Christians meeting in small fellowship groups in their homes. This practice worked for several years. It was inevitable, however, that conflicts would arise with the Jewish religious leaders. This led to persecution, the scattering of the church, and the development of other expressions of local congregations.

2. *Christian synagogues.* The missionary journeys of Paul in conjunction with Barnabas, Silas, Timothy, and others, led to the formation of local congregations in the provinces of Asia Minor. Many of these congregations were founded on a nucleus of Jewish converts who came

The Organizational Life of the Church

**Figure 15**

**Local Missional Congregations**

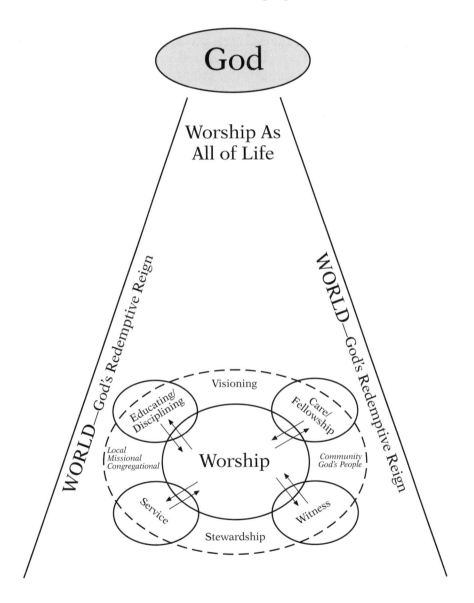

from local synagogues. The worship and leadership practices that became common to these local congregations followed the pattern of synagogues. This allowed for the mixing of Gentile and Jewish converts into a common community that had continuity with Judaism while being contextual within the Greek and Roman cultures.

3. *House congregations.* There was a fairly common practice of house churches being formed as a result of the gospel spreading throughout the Mediterranean world. Examples of these can be found woven into the various letters of Paul and others. We find, for example, churches that met in Lydia's house in Philippi (Acts 16:14–15); Gaius's house in Corinth (Rom. 16:23); Stephanas' house in Corinth (1 Cor. 16:15); Aquila and Priscilla's house in Ephesus (1 Cor. 16:19); Aristobulus' house and Narcissus' house in Rome (Rom. 16:10–11); and Archippus' house (Philem. 1:2) and Nympha's house in Colossae (Col. 4:15). It appears that many of these house churches functioned as extended households, which represented the common social structure within Roman society.[9]

4. *Collective city congregations.* The emergence of the church in cities like Antioch, Ephesus, Corinth, and Rome gave birth to another form of local congregation. While the information available is limited for defining the full character of these churches, there is enough evidence to draw a basic picture. Similar to the Jerusalem experience, but without the temple being available, Christians within these larger cities appear to have joined together in some form of collective life. Accompanying this larger assembling of believers were a variety of local congregations that met primarily in homes.

Three characteristics of local congregations are important to understanding the church's organizational life. First, local congregations are inherently missional. This reflects the church's apostolicity. In being missionary by nature, local congregations seek to reach beyond themselves into their local

The Organizational Life of the Church

areas to bear witness to the reign of God and to invite others into the community of faith.

Second, local congregations are to be bilingual in their communal life. This reflects the church's catholicity. Congregations are responsible to learn the language of faith because they are created by the Spirit. But they are also responsible to learn the language of their specific settings because they are contextual.

Third, local congregations are inherently connectional. They seek to be dynamically related to one another because each holds an identity of being part of the much larger visible church in the world. This reflects the church's oneness. For this to take place, local congregations will develop structures and processes to provide for relationship formation, communication, and common action. Much of this work is done through mobile missional structures.

### Mobile Missional Structures

Mobile missional structures complement local missional congregations.[10] They exist beyond congregations, yet their reason for existence and their ministry activities are intertwined with the life and ministry of congregations.

The visible church needs to be rooted in local settings. Local missional congregations meet this need. The visible church also needs to expand the ministry of the gospel into new areas, while contributing to cooperation and coordination between congregations. This is the work of the mobile missional structures (see fig. 16).

Several kinds of mobile missional structures are found in the New Testament.

1. *Apostolic leaders.* The first, and most important, of the mobile missional structures was the band of followers Jesus selected and trained as his apostles. This apostolic team was given the responsibility by Jesus to take the message of the gospel to the ends of the earth and to form communities of disciples as it did so. This group of leaders provided the early church with teaching that became

The Organizational Life of the Church

**Figure 16**

**Mobile Missional Structure**

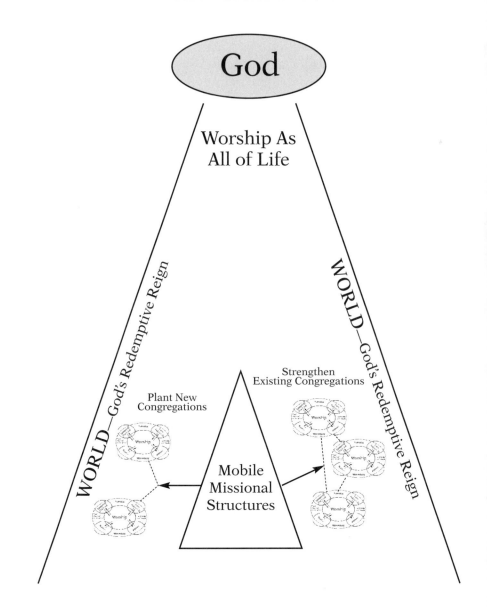

authoritative for the life of the church. This group of leaders also lived out of a mandate of sentness that became normative for the ministry of the church.

2. *Mobile team.* As the Spirit led the church into new areas, persons were selected by the apostles, by leaders appointed by the apostles, and by the leaders of local congregations to engage in the special work of spreading the gospel to new areas. Such activity is seen in the ministry of Barnabas to Antioch, of Barnabas and Paul to Asia Minor, and later of Paul, Silas, and Timothy to the same area. Over time, many leaders were added to this work, with most being given to this ministry by local congregations. We find, for example, Luke (Acts 16:10 ff); Titus (2 Cor. 8:16); Sopater, Aristarchus, Secundus, Gaius, Tychicus, Trophimus (Acts 20:4); and Epaphroditus (Phil. 2:25). In addition to the twelve apostles, at least twenty-eight named persons from at least fourteen different local congregations participated with these mobile teams.[11] Their work was threefold: strengthening local congregations, providing for coordinated ministry between congregations, and extending the gospel into new areas.

3. *At-large leaders.* Several persons who appear in the New Testament story of the expansion of the church had ministries related to the missional teams, but seemed to operate somewhat independently from the direct oversight of these teams. Examples include Philip (Acts 8–9), Apollos (Acts 18:24–19:1; 1 Cor. 1:12), and Priscilla and Aquila (Acts 18:26; Rom. 16:3–4). It appears that the ministries of such persons resulted from the exercise of their spiritual gifts and the willingness of the local congregations to receive them.

Three characteristics of mobile missional structures are important to note. First, mobile structures always exist in relation to local congregations, reflecting the church's oneness. They draw their personnel and resources from these congregations, and much of their work is related to the development and strengthening of these congregations.

Second, mobile structures are made up of leaders who have gifts and skills for broader ministry in the church, as well as training and experience in local ministry. These leaders often function as representatives of their local congregations.

Third, mobile structures function in many ways as specialized communities of believers. While these leaders were accountable to local communities, they often lived as a community among themselves to carry out their specialized ministry role.

These specialized communities of mobile missional structures worked for the development and expansion of the church in the New Testament world. They cooperated with local congregations, even while expanding the church into new areas that had not yet been reached. It is important, however, to clarify the interrelationship that developed between the local missional congregations and the mobile missional structures.

## Connectional Processes and Assembly

It was John's first time to serve as an elder-delegate at the presbytery meeting. A year ago, he had been elected to serve on the session of Springdale Presbyterian Church. He and Pastor Randy sat together along with about sixty other people in the auditorium of another Presbyterian Church where the meeting was being held. Following the roll call and reading of the correspondence, the moderator turned to an item that they had agreed to make the order of the day.

Presbytery was being asked by the General Assembly to vote on whether to support two resolutions related to human sexuality and ordained ministry. John had received a packet of materials with background information on these resolutions, but had not had time to work through it. A motion was offered to support the first resolution, and the debate began. As the process unfolded, John thought, "This really seems to be an important issue, but I don't feel very prepared to discuss it. Are we really in a position to vote on what we think the Bible teaches about this? I guess that's why it's mostly pastor-delegates who are rising to speak."

All churches must develop structures and processes for making decisions about important matters of doctrine and applying these decisions to the practices of church life. How are such matters to be decided? What authority do these decisions have in the lives of congregations and their members?

In considering connectional processes, we move from formulating a doctrine of the church to developing a polity for the church. We move from what is confessional for the church as a whole, to that which is conditioned by specific contexts. While broad principles for shaping a polity can be discerned, care must be taken not to absolutize particular cultural forms and make them normative for the church as a whole.[12]

Church polity has traditionally been developed around three theories of church government—congregational, presbyterian, and episcopal. While these distinctions are helpful, they tend to reflect the concerns of the Protestant Reformation—what constitutes the true, institutional church and the proper development of offices in this church. While these are important matters, others also need to be considered. A review of the various connectional processes developed in the early church offers a useful starting point.

## New Testament Precedents

In the early church, local missional congregations and mobile missional structures had to find ways to maintain unity while carrying out their respective ministries. Both organizational forms took initiative to accomplish this, although the greater initiative was exercised, as might be expected, by the mobile missional structures.

First, mobile structures took initiative to develop, strengthen, and supervise the life of local congregations. One example is the formation of the church in Jerusalem under the leadership of the original apostles. But a clearer example is seen in the work of the evolving mission team associated with Paul's three missionary journeys. On these journeys, there is a consistent pattern of the mobile structure bringing local congregations into existence. Most of these soon had leaders appointed for them by the mobile teams, leaders who were to guide the on-going life and ministries of these congregations.

This initiative was not limited, however, to the formation of new congregations. Later we find mobile structure personnel being assigned to strengthen existing congregations, as seen in the work of Timothy in Ephesus (1 Timothy) and Titus on the island of Crete (see Titus 1:5). We also find mobile structures helping local congregations take collective action, as when Paul's team took up the collection from congregations in Macedonia on behalf of the Jewish congregations who were experiencing famine (2 Corinthians 8).

Second, local congregations took initiative to launch and support mobile structures, and continued to monitor their work. The most obvious example of this was the Antioch congregation's forming and sending the mobile team of Barnabas and Saul on the first missionary journey. While both men were themselves imports into this church, they evidently felt accountable to report to this church on their work. As noted earlier, other congregations provided experienced personnel to the mobile structures. The giving of these persons to the work of the mobile structures apparently functioned as a type of thank offering for the work carried out by the mission team in their midst (e.g., see Epaphroditus in Phil. 2:25–30).

When a significant difference emerged between the initiatives taken by local congregations and mobile structures, it was resolved through a shared assembly. Acts 15 provides an account of the Jerusalem council. The controversy concerned the practice of circumcision in relation to the nature of the gospel. Paul and Barnabas, along with some other leaders from the Antioch congregation, were sent to the congregation in Jerusalem (v. 2), where "the apostles and elders met together to consider this matter" (v. 6). The solution agreed upon was considered valid for both the Jewish and Gentile congregations (vv. 22–29).

It is significant that representative leaders of both mobile structures and local congregations met in council and rendered this decision. It was critical for the emerging church to maintain a common faith and to come to a shared agree-

174

ment on how to apply this faith to a critical issue of the day. This necessitated the practice we have come to know as assembly.

The material in the New Testament that speaks directly to the development of connectional processes and assembly in the visible church is sketchy. What appears is a church being created by the Spirit that organizationally adapted itself to its context. While their purpose for adopting certain forms and practices is clear, the specifics of what they looked like and how they functioned are often left unclarified. Organization in the visible church, though critically important and normative in relation to its purpose, needs to be understood primarily in functional terms in relation to particular forms.

## Developing a Church Polity

The church as a social community needs to engage in shared practices in order for there to be meaning and direction in its corporate life. In the New Testament church, two types of shared processes can be seen. One focused on the development

**Figure 17**

**Connectional Processes and Assembly**

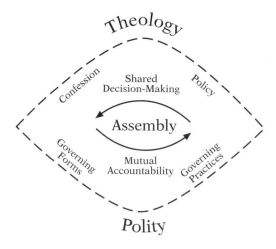

of content, while the other focused on the exercise of governance. As these processes unfolded, it was essential for the church to maintain unity. A shared assembly was developed for this purpose. This combination of connectional processes and a shared assembly make up the substance of what we have come to know as church polity (see fig. 17).

### Processes That Develop Content

The church being led by the Spirit and governed by the Word is always seeking to define its beliefs and apply these to its life and ministry. On the one hand, this leads to the practice of confession to help clarify what the church believes. On the other hand, the teaching of the Spirit guides the church in applying its beliefs to the concrete issues of its day, that is, in making policy decisions.

*Confession.* The church, in being created, led, and taught by the Spirit, will of necessity be a confessing church. By nature both one and many, it seeks to affirm those truths that are held in common. This is critical to the church's maintaining its essential unity.

It is natural for the church to develop particular confessions as it engages in this process. To do this, the church must interpret Scripture. The Bible comes to us as a story told through a variety of different genres. While there is continuity and cohesiveness within this story, there is also great diversity and development of thought. It is the responsibility of the church, under the leading and teaching of the Spirit, to discern and define the truths woven through the whole of the story.

The decision of the Jerusalem council is an example of the church working to define the content of the gospel. In addition, the New Testament includes some evidence of early confessional forms.[13] These forms were developed and used by both local congregations and mobile structures to summarize the essential truths of the apostolic tradition. Some appear to speak to specific problems that were emerging in the life of the church. The development of confessions has continued to be a dynamic part of the historical church. The church that is being

The Organizational Life of the Church

led and taught by the Spirit will be a confessing church, but it is important to remember that particular confessions are always context-shaped.

*Policy Decisions.* The church, being by nature catholic, and therefore contextual, seeks to make discerning policy decisions about specific cultural issues. Some of these issues affect the well-being of the church as a whole, the catholic church. Other problems confront local congregations within specific contexts. In both cases, the church must apply its understanding of biblical teaching to these issues. At times, the historical confessions provide guidance. At other times, the church needs to engage in a fresh study of Scripture to bring light to bear on the issues.

Making policy decisions is an important process in the life of the church. This can be seen in how the decision of the Jerusalem council was applied to the Gentile context with sensitivity to Jewish concerns.[14] Wise policy decisions strengthen the life of the church. In addition, they are crucial for the church's participation in the redemptive reign of God and its role in unmasking the powers. Policy decisions shape the corporate commitments and behaviors of God's people. As God's people seek to live consistent with these policy decisions, the church is strengthened and the redemptive power of God is displayed to a lost and broken world.

## Processes for Governing

Just as the church develops processes to define and apply its understanding of truth, it also develops processes to organize its life as a social community. The church develops patterned behaviors for governing its life. These make up the operational side of church polity.

*Governing Forms.* While specific forms are contextually shaped, they are not arbitrary. They must be carefully considered in light of biblical foundations and historical developments. Governing forms locate God's power and authority within church life through various leadership positions and decision-making structures.

In the New Testament, we find leadership roles lodged in such positions as apostles, prophets, evangelists, pastor-teachers, bishops, elders, and deacons. We find these leaders working within a variety of decision-making structures, such as the apostolic circle, the seven additional leaders in Jerusalem, the leadership teams of mobile mission personnel, elder groups ruling local congregations, deacons ministering in local congregations, and the Jerusalem council.[15]

The governing forms of leadership positions and decision-making structures connect the power and presence of the Spirit in the corporate life of the church with the lives of individual participants. The evidence of the New Testament suggests that the variety found in these forms indicates their developmental character. Yet the particular forms found there also represented God's authority in the life of the church. Because of this, governing forms often take on important symbolic meanings.

We need to be careful that a governing form does not become an end in itself. The form is intended to serve the church in carrying out ministry consistent with its nature. At the same time, we must be good stewards of the power of God represented in these forms.

*Governing Practices.* The church must develop some shared procedures related to leadership positions and decision-making structures. Governing practices, like governing forms, must be contextual, functional, and flexible. The New Testament presents a picture of a church that continued to shape its governing practices in conjunction with its growth and the new contexts it encountered.

Governing practices should promote unity in the church. Achieving unity, however, does not require uniform practices. The church can maintain unity even while developing a wide range of practices for implementing the same aspect of ministry, as long as there is a submission to the principle of being governed by the Word as it is led and taught by the Spirit. To carry out ministry consistent with its nature, the church must maintain a developmental and contextual understanding of both governing forms and governing practices. This requires the

The Organizational Life of the Church

church to function on the basis of broad principles that allow for flexibility within different contexts. However, differences will emerge that need to be addressed. The New Testament church provides a precedent for how to proceed when this occurs.

## Assembly

If the church is to maintain its unity and continue to grow, it must come to agreement when issues emerge that need to be resolved. It must also maintain mutual accountability among leaders.

*Assembly Provides for Shared Decision-Making.* The Jerusalem council functioned as a shared assembly of leaders from both local congregations and mobile structures. Its purpose was to render a confessional understanding of the content of the gospel, and to apply it through a policy decision to the contextual needs of the church. The representative leaders of local congregations and mobile structures need to share in decision-making. These two structures complement one another in carrying out the mission of God in the world.

*Assembly Provides for Mutual Accountability.* In making and implementing the decision reached at the Jerusalem council, the representative leaders of local congregations and mobile structures exercised mutual accountability. This is reflected in the support given by all parties to the decision reached in Acts 15. It is also evident in the reporting of Barnabas and Paul, and later Paul and Silas, to the church in Antioch regarding their work. This accountability helped the church maintain a balance between global and local concerns.

For the church to carry its ministry to the ends of the earth, it must have both local and mobile structures. Local missional congregations are needed for living out the redemptive purposes of God in specific contexts. Mobile missional structures are needed to carry the message of redemption to new locations and strengthen local congregations. Between these two kinds of structures there must be such connectional processes as shared decision-making and mutual accountability among the leaders.

179

# Leadership in the Church

It was a painful experience for Springdale Baptist. Pastor Tom had been a dynamic leader and effective preacher, but he had gotten involved in a sexual indiscretion while counseling a female member. When the board of deacons approached him on the matter, Pastor Tom agreed to resign. The board was now trying to find another pastor.

As the search committee met, Bob spoke up, "We need to spend some time grieving our loss and being honest with the congregation about Tom's betrayal of us all."

Sam responded, "It's over and finished and we just need to move on. We don't need to keep dragging this issue up before the congregation. There's been enough hurt already."

Bob countered, "I don't want to drag anything on. I just think we need to be honest with our hurt."

As the discussion continued, the conversation turned to criteria to consider in selecting a new pastor. Several expressed reservations about getting someone else with Tom's strong leadership skills. "After all," said John, "maybe our relying so much on Tom's abilities contributed to his problem." Mary suggested another approach. "Perhaps we need someone who has good skills in pastoral care and shepherding. Maybe that could help us get past what we are going through."

Leadership is a critical aspect of the organizational life of the church. What abilities are needed? How do abilities relate to character? How are we to understand abilities and character in relation to the office of pastor? What exactly does office and ordination mean in the life of the church? These are important questions.

Leaders in the church help people live together as a community. Their influence comes partly from the stability their positions provide. It comes partly from the specific gifts and abilities they bring to their work. But foundational to church leadership is forming relationships. Christian ministry is inherently relational. The relationships among church leaders in particular are a critical aspect of the Spirit's work in creating a missional community.

While many of the qualifications for church leadership parallel those of other organizations, some leadership requirements are unique to the church. The importance of qualified and trained leadership is clear from the attention Jesus gave to selecting and preparing the twelve apostles. As the early church grew, it had to formulate criteria for the selection of its leaders.

## Leaders with Character and Gifts

The biblical story is filled with teaching and illustrative material about leadership in the community of God's people. In the Old Testament, this leadership functioned primarily through the offices of prophet, priest, and king, although some provided leadership apart from these formal roles. In the New Testament, leadership functioned in a variety of roles both in local congregations and mobile structures. The biblical teaching on leadership emphasizes two categories of qualifications.

First, leaders in the church must have a mature Christian character. Anyone who is going to be a leader in the church must demonstrate maturity in exercising the fruit of the Spirit (Gal. 5:22–23). This fruit is mostly social in character in the sense that these behaviors function primarily in relationship to other persons. To be a leader in the church, a person must demonstrate the ability to develop mature relationships with other believers.

Second, the Bible assumes that leaders in the church will be selected based on their gifts and skills. The Spirit gives spiritual gifts to all in the church. Some gifts relate directly to leadership. It is the Spirit who prompts, motivates, and energizes a person with the appropriate gifts to exercise a leadership role. The church is responsible to confirm those who have the gifts and skills for leadership. The calling of leaders is a social process. Other leaders identify, recruit, train, and test those who might serve as additional leaders (e.g., see 2 Cor. 8:22). The whole community confirms those who have been selected.

181

## Leaders As Gifts

*really?*

The Bible assumes church leaders will be credentialed in some formal manner. This credentialing does not confer spiritual empowerment. Spiritual empowerment is a function of spiritual fruit being mature and spiritual gifts being developed. Credentialing is a formal confirmation that such fruit and gifts are already present. It is critical to keep this relationship in the proper order. There is always a danger of the formal role displacing a proper emphasis on fruit and gifts. The church must develop and employ processes that safeguard the proper order.

In Ephesians 4, Paul says that certain leaders in the church are to be seen, in themselves, as gifts from God to the church. In the church, leaders do not take leadership upon themselves. They are called by the Spirit and selected for leadership roles in the Spirit's working through the community of faith. They are empowered for their ministry roles by the Spirit, and they minister within the body consistent with the spiritual gifts given to them by the Spirit. From beginning to end, leaders in the church function on a different basis from secular leadership. They display the same human behaviors, but from a different motivation, from a different source of power, and for different reasons.

## Leaders in Gift–Shaped Ministries

Leadership in the church is gift-shaped. In Ephesians 4 and 1 Corinthians 12:28, a number of speaking gifts are related to roles the Spirit uses to equip and strengthen those in the church. Priority is given to apostles, prophets, evangelists, teachers, and pastor-teachers. This variety of roles reflects specific spiritual gifts given to individuals, who are themselves to be seen within these roles as gifts to the church. The focus is not on any position held, but on the ministry to be carried out consistent with the gift-shaped character of the role. Leadership positions in the church exist for the purpose of ministry, even while these positions represent God's authority in the life of the church.

The Bible makes this clear in the term that is used to talk about ministry roles, a word best translated as "service" or "min-

The Organizational Life of the Church

istry."[16] This same word has come into common usage in the church today as "office." The focus in the Bible is not so much on an office and the authority one possesses, but rather on the service and ministry responsibilities one is to carry out. This means that power in the church is social and collective by nature, rather than personal and private. Possessing and controlling power is never the prerogative of an individual.

The leaders in the New Testament church who functioned in gift-shaped ministries (offices) seem to have served primarily the needs of the broader church. They were most often found in the mobile missional structures that helped establish and strengthen local congregations. This is clearly true of the roles of apostle, prophet, teacher, and evangelist. The role of pastor-teacher in Ephesians 4:11 has often been exegeted as referring to a full-time leader of a local congregation.[17] Typically cited as evidence for support of this is the functioning of Timothy in Ephesus. The work of Timothy, however, appears to be that of a mobile person carrying out responsibilities assigned by the mission team he served. The healthy development and functioning of local missional congregations often required the effective functioning of such persons.

## Leadership within Role-Defined Ministries

Local congregations need leaders. The pattern that emerged in the New Testament was the appointment of elders to provide this leadership. This pattern appears to have followed the common practice of Jewish synagogues. As Christian synagogues were formed, elders from within each assembly were appointed, usually by mobile personnel. Little detail is provided on how these elders carried out their work, but clearly the emphasis was on providing effective rule in the life of the congregation. Those who labored as elders in teaching-preaching roles were worthy of double honor.

It appears that much of the teaching and preaching ministry required in the local congregations was initially done by mobile personnel, then increasingly taken over by elders in each congregation. The practice of one person functioning as a solo pastor within a local congregation does not appear to have been the normative pattern among these churches. What does emerge toward the end of the first century is the practice of one person emerging in the role of bishop within an urban area, following the structure common in Roman society.[18]

The New Testament describes a variety of approaches for identifying and placing leaders. It appears that the Spirit intended for the church to maintain flexibility as it continued to grow. Leadership practices will vary and continue to evolve in a growing and changing church.

## The Church in North America

It has been the argument of this book that we need to rethink the church from the framework of a missiological ecclesiology. I believe that it is only through such a framework that we can engage the complexity of the situation we now encounter in North America. For many of us, this complexity is overwhelming. It involves a tremendous diversity of organizational forms within the North American church, plus a dramatic shift that is taking place in our culture with the emergence of postmodernism. It is my prayer that those who read this book will find perspective and inspiration to engage this complexity through their own faith communities as these communities are led and taught by the Spirit.

184

# Notes

## Chapter 1: *Rediscovering the Church in the Twenty-First Century*

1. The suburban community of Springdale is a composite of many of the churches I have consulted with over the years and many of the communities where I have worked. All the illustrations reflect actual experiences in relation to these churches and their communities.

2. A helpful source that provides a numerical summary of denominational churches within each county in the United States is published every ten years by the Glenmary Research Center in Atlanta, Georgia. The most recent study is entitled *Churches and Church Membership in the United States 1990*, eds. Martin B. Bradley et al., 1992.

3. A recent study that documents this is Nancy T. Ammerman, *Congregation and Community* (New Brunswick, N.J.: Rutgers University Press, 1997).

4. Many of these denominations have rather small memberships. A helpful source for getting perspective on the history, doctrine, organization, and membership of denominations is Frank S. Mead, rev. Samuel S. Hill, *Handbook of Denominations in the United States*, 9th ed., (Nashville: Abingdon, 1990).

5. Martin E. Marty, *Righteous Empire* (New York: Dial Press, 1970), 67–68.

6. Russell E. Richey, "Denominations and Denominationalism: An American Morphology," in Robert B. Mullin and Russell E. Richey, eds., *Reimagining Denominationalism* (New York: Oxford University Press, 1994), 74–98.

7. A discussion of these various approaches is provided by Craig Van Gelder, "Missional Challenge: Understanding the Church in North America," in Darrell L. Guder, ed., *Missional Church: A Theological Vision for the Sending of the Church in North America* (Grand Rapids: Eerdmans, 1998), 67–72.

8. For a treatment of the formation of the modern denomination with its agency structures see Elwyn A. Smith, "The Forming of a Modern American Denomination," in Russell E. Richey, ed., *Denominationalism* (Nashville: Abingdon, 1977), 108–36.

9. A helpful treatment of the history and development of special purpose groups within the Christian movement is provided in Robert Wuthnow, *The*

*Restructuring of American Religion* (Princeton, N.J.: Princeton University Press, 1988), 100–31.

10. Van Gelder, "Missional Challenge," 67–72.

11. A discussion of the relationship of internal and external factors on local congregation growth can be found in Wade Clark Roof et al., "Factors Producing Growth or Decline in United Presbyterian Congregations," in Dean R. Hoge and David A. Roozen, eds., *Understanding Church Growth and Decline 1950–1978* (New York: Pilgrim, 1979), 198–247.

12. The discussion of postmodernism is quite complex. Some recent publications which offer perspective on this phenomenon include: Steven Best and Douglas Kellner, *Postmodern Theory* (New York: Guilford, 1991); Steven Connor, *Postmodernist Culture* (Cambridge, Mass.: Basil Blackwell, 1989); Stanley J. Grenz, *A Primer on Postmodernism* (Grand Rapids: Eerdmans, 1996); Robert Hollinger, *Postmodernism and the Social Sciences* (Thousand Oaks, Calif.: Sage Publications, 1994); and J. Richard Middleton and Brian J. Walsh, *Truth Is Stranger Than It Used to Be* (Downers Grove, Ill.: InterVarsity, 1995).

13. A fuller discussion of this can be found in Van Gelder, "Missional Challenge," 72–73.

14. Recent books which present these various themes are: George G. Hunter III, *Church for the Unchurched* (Nashville: Abingdon, 1996); Rick Warren, *The Purpose Driven Church* (Grand Rapids: Zondervan, 1995); Carl F. George, *Prepare Your Church for the Future* (Tarrytown, N.Y.: Revell, 1991); George Barna, *User Friendly Churches* (Ventura, Calif.: Regal, 1991); Lyle E. Schaller, *The Seven-Day-a-Week Church* (Nashville: Abingdon, 1992); and Leith Anderson, *A Church for the 21st Century* (Minneapolis: Bethany House, 1992).

15. Recent publications emphasizing these themes are: Wuthnow, *The Restructuring of American Religion*; Nancy T. Ammerman et al., eds., *Studying Congregations: A New Handbook* (Nashville: Abingdon, 1998); David A. Roozen and C. Kirk Hadaway, *Church and Denominational Growth* (Nashville: Abingdon, 1993); Mullin and Richey, eds., *Reimagining Denominationalism*; Norman Shawchuck and Gustave Rath, *Benchmarks of Quality in the Church* (Nashville: Abingdon, 1994); and Daniel A. Brown, *The Other Side of Pastoral Ministry* (Grand Rapids: Zondervan, 1996).

16. The concept of the "next" church was recently popularized by Charles Trueheart, "Welcome to the Next Church," *The Atlantic Monthly*, August 1996, 37–58.

17. While many sources address this theme, one perspective gaining increasing importance discusses the church in relationship to gospel and culture themes. Examples of this literature include: Lesslie Newbigin, *Foolishness to the Greeks* (Grand Rapids: Eerdmans, 1986); and Stanley Hauerwas and William H. Willimon, *Resident Aliens* (Nashville: Abingdon, 1989).

18. This perspective is critical to understand in treating the church. While dated in some ways, the treatment by Hans Kung, *The Church* (New York:

186

Sheed and Ward, 1967), 3–39, still serves as an excellent introduction to this shift in ecclesiological studies.

## Chapter 2: *A Missional Understanding of the Church*

1. The connection between obedience to the Great Commission and the formation of specialized mission structures to carry out this work is found in William Carey, the father of modern missions, in his seminal treatise, *An Enquiry into the Obligations of Christians to Use Means for the Conversion of the Heathens* (London: Hodder and Stoughton, 1792).

2. A example of this approach to missions is found in Earl Parvin, *Missions USA* (Chicago: Moody, 1985).

3. While many evangelism methodologies have been developed and promoted over the past several decades, the one that has perhaps had the most influence is D. James Kennedy, *Evangelism Explosion* (Wheaton: Tyndale, 1970). The emphases on personal responsibility, specialized training, and the use of a prescribed methodology are all deeply imbedded in this approach.

4. Probably the most familiar example of this distinction in missiology circles is found in the decision in 1969 by the Commission on World Mission and Evangelism of the World Council of Churches to change the title of its quarterly journal from *International Review of Missions* to *International Review of Mission*. The dropping of the *s* signaled an important shift in understanding the biblical and theological foundations of God's work in the world through the church.

5. The recent book by Charles Van Engen, *Mission on the Way* (Grand Rapids: Baker, 1996), 148–56, illustrates this dilemma of treating church and mission as two separate entities. By framing his discussion in these terms, Van Engen tends to set up a dichotomy that is difficult to overcome.

6. Two recent examples of an effort to achieve a common framework have come out of the Gospel and Our Culture Network movement in North America: George R. Hunsberger and Craig Van Gelder, *The Church Between Gospel and Culture: The Emerging Mission in North America* (Grand Rapids: Eerdmans, 1996); and Guder, ed., *Missional Church*.

7. J. Verkuyl, *Contemporary Missiology: An Introduction* (Grand Rapids: Eerdmans, 1978), 26–88.

8. As illustrated earlier in Carey, *Enquiry*.

9. A helpful discussion of this development is found in Van Engen, *Mission on the Way*, 17–31. This distinction is also treated by David J. Bosch, *Transforming Mission: Paradigm Shifts in Theology of Mission* (Maryknoll, N.Y.: Orbis, 1991), 15–16.

10. Bosch, *Transforming Mission*, 492–94.

11. An older, but still relevant, introduction to this orientation is Herman Ridderbos, *The Coming of the Kingdom* (Philadelphia: Presbyterian and Reformed Publishing Co., 1962).

12. These include the Vatican II documents, "Dogmatic Constitution on the Church" *(Lumen Gentium)*, 1964, and "Decree on the Church's Missionary Activity" *(Ad Gentes)*, 1965; in addition to CELAM II, the Second General Conference of Latin American Bishops held at Medellin, Colombia in 1968; and CELAM III, the Third General Conference of Latin American Bishops held at Puebla, Mexico in 1979.

13. This papal document titled "Apostolic Exhortation" *(Evangelii Nuntiandi)*, 1975, was translated into English as "The Evangelization of the Men of Our Time," (Washington, D.C.: United States Catholic Conference, 1976).

14. An important document which developed this perspective was written in anticipation of this merger by Lesslie Newbigin, *One Body, One Gospel, One World* (London and New York: International Missionary Council, 1958).

15. See especially Johannes Blauw, *The Missionary Nature of the Church* (Grand Rapids: Eerdmans, 1962).

16. Of special significance is the 1982 publication by the Commission on World Mission and Evangelism of the study, "Mission and Evangelism: An Ecumenical Affirmation," which can be found in *International Review of Mission* 71, no. 284 (October 1982): 427–51.

17. An example of the growing influence of this perspective can be seen in the consultation convened in Grand Rapids in 1982 by the Theological Working Group of the Lausanne Committee on World Evangelization. This report is "No. 21: Grand Rapids Report—Evangelism and Social Responsibility, An Evangelical Commitment," *Lausanne Occasional Papers* (Lausanne Committee for World Evangelization and World Evangelical Fellowship, 1982).

18. A summary of these developments is provided by Kevin Giles, *What on Earth Is the Church?* (Downers Grove, Ill.: InterVarsity, 1995), 212–29.

19. An introduction to the Pentecostal perspective on this subject is found in Section I, "Biblical and Theological Dimensions of Global Mission in the Pentecostal Tradition," in Murray A. Dempter et al., *Called and Empowered: Global Mission in Pentecostal Perspective* (Peabody, Mass.: Hendrickson, 1991), 1–38.

20. This shift is treated at length in Kung, *The Church;* and is also reviewed in Avery Dulles, *Models of the Church* (New York: Doubleday, Image Books, 1974 [1987]).

21. A treatment of this subject is found in Guillermo Cook, *The Expectation of the Poor: Latin American Basic Ecclesial Communities in Protestant Perspective* (Maryknoll, N.Y.: Orbis, 1985). See also Leonardo Boff, *Ecclesiogenesis: The Base Communities Reinvent the Church* (Maryknoll, N.Y.: Orbis, 1986).

22. Blauw, *The Missionary Nature of the Church.*

23. A historical treatment of these developments is found in William Richey Hogg, *Ecumenical Foundations* (New York: Harper and Brothers, 1952).

24. Giles, *What on Earth Is the Church?*

25. Representative literature from this movement includes Lawrence O. Richards, *A New Face for the Church* (Grand Rapids: Zondervan, 1970); David R. Mains, *Full Circle* (Waco: Word, 1971); and Gene A. Getz, *Sharpening the Focus of the Church* (Chicago: Moody, 1974).

26. A great number of publications have been written by persons working within the church growth movement. Some representative examples include Donald A. McGavran, *Understanding Church Growth* (Grand Rapids: Eerdmans, 1970); Virgil Gerber, *A Manual for Evangelism/Church Growth* (South Pasadena, Calif.: Wm. Carey Library, 1973); Win Arn, ed., *The Pastor's Church Growth Handbook* (Pasadena, Calif.: Church Growth Press, 1979); Ebbie C. Smith, *Balanced Church Growth* (Nashville: Broadman, 1984); and C. Peter Wagner, *Strategies for Church Growth* (Ventura, Calif.: Regal, 1987).

27. The concept of organizational effectiveness comes from the behavioral sciences. This emphasis has gained importance within organizational studies in recent years. While not many church-related authors develop a thoroughgoing theory of organizational effectiveness, evidences of its influence can be seen running throughout much of the recent literature. See for example: Kennon L. Callahan, *Effective Church Leadership* (New York: Harper and Row, 1990); and Norman Shawchuck and Roger Heuser, *Leading the Congregation* (Nashville: Abingdon, 1993).

28. Guder, *Missional Church.*

29. Examples of this approach can be found in such recent publications as: David W. Hall and Joseph H. Hall, eds., *Paradigms in Polity* (Grand Rapids: Eerdmans, 1994); and Edmund P. Clowney, *The Church: Contours of Christian Theology* (Downers Grove, Ill.: InterVarsity, 1995).

30. An example of this can be found in Wagner, *Strategies for Church Growth,* 29–32.

31. A study, which has come to be accepted as a classic, that worked out some of the implications of these various approaches is H. Richard Niebuhr, *Christ and Culture* (New York: Harper, 1951).

32. A good summary of the development and use of this concept in missiological circles is found in Bosch, *Transforming Mission,* 420–32. See also Paul G. Hiebert, "Critical Contextualization," in *International Bulletin of Missionary Research* 11, no. 3 (July 1987): 104–12; and Darrell L. Whiteman, "Contextualization: The Theory, the Gap, the Challenge," in *International Bulletin of Missionary Research* 21, no. 1 (January 1997): 2–7. A recent effort to apply this perspective to the formulation of an ecclesiology is Johannes A. van der Ven, *Ecclesiology in Context* (Grand Rapids: Eerdmans, [1993] 1996).

33. See Craig Van Gelder, "Missional Challenge," 48–60.

## Chapter 3: *Historical Views of the Church*

1. This was a common approach by some authors in the 1960s who sought to discredit what they felt were limiting concepts developed within the Reformation tradition. See, for example: Harry R. Boer, *Pentecost and Missions*

(Grand Rapids: Eerdmans, 1961); J. C. Hoekendijk, *The Church Inside Out* (Philadelphia: Westminster, 1964); and John H. Piet, *The Road Ahead: A Theology for the Church in Mission* (Grand Rapids: Eerdmans, 1970).

2. A brief discussion of this council and the creed which resulted from it can be found in John H. Leith, ed., *Creeds and Confessions* (Richmond: John Knox, 1973), 31–33.

3. Ibid., 22–26.

4. A discussion of how the four attributes came to describe the Roman Catholic Church can be found in Kung, *The Church*, 261–359.

5. A recent effort to draw out these implications has been made by Charles Van Engen, *God's Missionary People* (Grand Rapids: Baker, 1991), 59–71; and Van Engen, *Mission on the Way*, 115–24.

6. Kung, *The Church*, 266 and 338–339.

7. A brief discussion of the background to this confession along with a copy of its content can be found in Leith, *Creeds and Confessions*, 63–107.

8. A brief discussion of the background to this confession and a copy of its content can be found in *Psalter Hymnal* (Grand Rapids: CRC Publications, 1987), 817–59.

9. None of the confessions that became the official confessional standards within the Lutheran, Reformed, and Anglican traditions directly use this attribute to describe the church.

10. The Lutheran Church was established as the state church first in Germany and later in most Baltic and Scandinavian countries; branches of the Reformed Church were established as state churches in Scotland and Holland; and the Anglican Church was established as the state church in England.

11. This emphasis can be seen in the introductory article of the "Ecclesiastical Ordinances" developed by John Calvin in 1561; see Hall and Hall, *Paradigms in Polity*, 140–41. It can also be found in the first article of "The Church Order of Dordt"; see Hall and Hall, *Paradigms in Polity*, 176.

12. Peter C. Hodgson, *Revisioning the Church* (Minneapolis: Fortress, 1988), 45.

13. A brief discussion of the background to this confession and a copy of its content can be found in Leith, *Creeds and Confessions*, 192–230.

14. This process of conservative groups removing themselves from parent denominations accused of becoming liberal has been common in this century. Examples include the formation of the General Association of Regular Baptist Churches in 1932 which withdrew from the American Baptist Convention; the formation of the Orthodox Presbyterian Church in 1936 which withdrew from the Presbyterian Church in the U.S.A.; and the more recent withdrawal of the Presbyterian Church in America from the Presbyterian Church U.S. in the 1970s. A variation on this theme was experienced by both the Lutheran Church Missouri Synod in the 1970s and the Southern Baptist Convention in the 1980 and 90s, where groups which held more moderate viewpoints chose (were forced) to leave their more conservative parent denominations.

15. A brief discussion of the background to this confession and a copy of its content can be found in Leith, *Creeds and Confessions*, 292–308.

16. A helpful discussion of Zinzendorf's views can be found in A. T. Lewis, *Zinzendorf the Ecumenical Pioneer* (London: SCM, 1962).

17. Ibid.

18. Carey, *Enquiry*, 82–83.

19. As discussed in Stephen Neill, *A History of Christian Missions* (New York: Penguin, 1964), 252. Examples include London Missionary Society (1795); Church Missionary Society (1799); British and Foreign Bible Society (1804); Basel Society (1815); Berlin Society (1824); and societies in Denmark (1821), France (1822), Sweden (1835), and Norway (1842).

20. A discussion of this can be found in Winthrop S. Hudson, *Religion in America* (New York: Charles Scribner's Sons, 1965), 150–57. The initial organizations were formed as cooperative ventures of the various denominations and included such groups as American Board of Commissioners for Foreign Missions (1810); American Bible Society (1816); American Education Society (1816); American Sunday School Union (1824); and American Tract Society (1826). As pointed out by Elwyn A. Smith, "The Forming of a Modern American Denomination," in Richey, *Denominationalism*, 133–36, by the 1830s most of the denominations, as illustrated by the Presbyterians, began to withdraw from the earlier cooperative efforts and form their own denominational boards and agencies.

21. Neill, *A History of Christian Missions*, 194–95.

22. This is the thesis developed by Winthrop S. Hudson, "Denominationalism as a Basis for Ecumenicity: A Seventeenth Century Conception," in Richey, *Denominationalism*, 21–42.

23. Richey, *Denominationalism*, 19–20; and Mullin and Richey, *Reimagining Denominationalism*, 3–11.

24. Marty, *Righteous Empire*, 67–68.

25. John Locke, "A Letter Concerning Toleration," in Maurice Cranston, ed., *Locke on Politics, Religion, and Education* (New York: Collier, 1965), 110–11.

26. Hudson, *Religion in America*, 109–30.

27. John Webster Grant, *The Church in the Canadian Era* (Toronto, Ontario: McGraw-Hill Ryerson, 1972), 1–23.

28. E. Franklin Frazier, *The Negro Church in America* (New York: Schocken, 1974), 35–51.

29. Ibid., 14, 36.

## Chapter 4: *The Church and the Redemptive Reign of God*

1. A recent publication that provides a summary of this diversity is Howard A. Snyder, *Models of the Kingdom* (Nashville: Abingdon, 1991).

2. The literature on this is extensive, but some important contributions include: Ridderbos, *The Coming of the Kingdom*, 334–96; Kung, *The Church*,

41–104; George Eldon Ladd, *A Theology of the New Testament* (Grand Rapids: Eerdmans, 1974), 105–19; Donald Senior and Carroll Stuhlmueller, *The Biblical Foundations for Mission* (Maryknoll, N.Y.: Orbis, 1983), 141–60; and Bosch, *Transforming Mission*, 31–35.

3. This emphasis is developed by George Hunsberger, "Missional Vocation: Called and Sent to Represent the Reign of God," in Guder, ed., *Missional Church*, 77–109.

4. Ridderbos, *The Coming of the Kingdom*, 24–27.

5. Snyder, *Models of the Kingdom*.

6. Ridderbos, *The Coming of the Kingdom*, 31–36.

7. Ibid., 163–69.

8. Ladd, *A Theology of the New Testament*, 36–40.

9. Kung, *The Church*, 70–79; and Bosch, *Transforming Mission*, 36–39.

10. Hunsberger, "Missional Vocation," 93–97.

11. See Giles, *What on Earth Is the Church?* 212–29; Jurgen Moltmann, *The Church in the Power of the Spirit* (Minneapolis: Fortress, [1975] 1993), 50–65; and Lesslie Newbigin, *The Open Secret* (Grand Rapids: Eerdmans, 1978), 20–31.

12. The language of the church functioning as sacrament, sign, and instrument was discussed by Dulles, *Models of the Church*, 63–75; and by Bosch, *Transforming Mission*, 374–76. In Newbigin, *The Open Secret*, 124, these concepts are discussed as sign, foretaste, and instrument.

## Chapter 5: *The Nature of the Church*

1. A discussion of the various names given to the early church is found in Giles, *What on Earth Is the Church?* 74–92.

2. See Kung, *The Church*, 34–39, and Giles, *What on Earth Is the Church?* 182–95.

3. Paul S. Minear, *Images of the Church in the New Testament* (Philadelphia: Westminster, 1960).

4. The study by Minear is helpful for establishing this theme; see also Kung, *The Church*, 1–39; Moltmann, *The Church in the Power of the Spirit*, 1–18; and Giles, *What on Earth Is the Church?* 1–25. Another important source that helped establish this thesis during the twentieth century is Dietrich Bonhoeffer in his work *Sanctorum Communio* that was translated into English as *The Communion of Saints: A Dogmatic Inquiry into the Sociology of the Church* (New York: Harpers, 1963).

5. Hodgson, *Revisioning the Church*, 29–30.

6. This theme has received new emphasis in the past few decades both through the expanding small group movement and the various processes that promote spiritual gift inventory. A theological perspective on these developments is provided by Greg Ogden, *The New Reformation: Returning the Ministry to the People of God* (Grand Rapids: Zondervan, 1990).

7. Of special importance was the conception of the modern man developed by Descartes who viewed persons as rational, autonomous individuals capable of making their own decisions, and the notion of social contract developed by Locke who conceived society as being the product of such rational, autonomous individuals choosing to live together within some form of contractual agreement.

8. Kung, *The Church*, 261–359.

9. Ibid., 30–34.

10. Ibid., 324.

11. See section in chapter 2 "Contextual Perspectives on the Church."

12. This thesis is developed by Lamin Sanneh, *Translating the Message: The Missionary Impact on Culture* (Maryknoll, N.Y.: Orbis, 1993).

13. Kung, *The Church*, 344–59.

14. Senior and Stuhlmueller, *The Biblical Foundations for Mission*, 266.

## Chapter 6: *The Ministry of the Church*

1. These emphases can be traced within the themes developed in the confessional standards which came to be adopted by the various Protestant churches in the sixteenth and seventeenth centuries.

2. Giles, *What on Earth Is the Church?* 212–29.

3. Sydney E. Ahlstrom, *A Religious History of the American People*, vol. 1 (Garden City, N.Y.: Image, 1975), 521–50.

4. Niebuhr, *Christ and Culture*.

5. This point is perhaps best illustrated in the three temptations Jesus faced early in his ministry as recorded in Matthew 4:1–11.

6. This perspective is often referred to as hyper-Calvinism. An interesting example of how this view of covenantal privilege can shape the identity of a people, sometimes in ways that have negative consequences for others, is the experience of the Dutch immigrants who settled in South Africa.

7. Kung, *The Church*, 319–44.

8. John T. McNeill, *The History and Character of Calvinism* (New York: Oxford University Press, 1954), 259–62.

9. Harvie E. Conn, *Eternal Word and Changing World: Theology, Anthropology, and Mission in Trialogue* (Grand Rapids: Zondervan, Academie Books, 1984), 211–60.

10. Sanneh, *Translating the Message*.

11. Colin Brown, ed., *The New International Dictionary of New Testament Theology*, vol. 3 (Grand Rapids: Zondervan, [1971] 1978), 549–51.

## Chapter 7: *The Organizational Life of the Church*

1. I intend to address this topic in future writing.

2. Neil J. Smelser, "Social Structure," in Neil J. Smelser, ed., *Handbook of Sociology* (Newbury Park, Calif.: Sage Publications, 1988), 125–26.

3. This has been a common theme in mission literature over the past century. Representative publications of this perspective include: John L. Nevius, *The Planting and Development of Missionary Churches* (Nutley, N.J.: Presbyterian and Reformed Publishing Co., [1886] 1958); Roland Allen, *Missionary Methods: St. Paul's or Ours?* (Grand Rapids: Eerdmans, [1927] 1962); and Melvin L. Hodges, *The Indigenous Church* (Springfield, Mo.: Gospel Publishing House, 1953).

4. As illustrated earlier in Hall and Hall, *Paradigms in Polity*.

5. As illustrated earlier in McGavran, *Understanding Church Growth*, and Wagner, *Strategies for Church Growth*.

6. Kung, *The Church*, 388–417.

7. F. Filson, *A New Testament History* (London: SCM, 1965), 345–48.

8. It would appear that many of the battles associated with today's "worship wars" are more matters of style and preference than issues of biblical principle or theology. For many persons, maintaining a certain tradition takes precedence over issues of context or function, even when there is limited biblical support for the particular forms of the tradition.

9. Del Birkey, *The House Church: A Model for Renewing the Church* (Scottdale, Pa.: Herald Press, 1988), 40–62.

10. This perspective is amplified in Ralph D. Winter, "The Two Structures of God's Redemptive Mission," in *Missiology: An International Review* 2, no. 1 (January 1974): 121–39.

11. These persons include Barnabas (Acts 11), John Mark (Acts 13–14; Col. 4:10), Judas and Silas (Acts 15:27) from Jerusalem; Paul from Tarsus; Timothy (Acts 16) from Lystra; Luke (Acts 16 ff.) most likely from Antioch; Gaius (Acts 20:4) from Derbe; Gaius (Acts 19:29) from Macedonia; Epaphras (Col. 4:12) and Onesimus (Philem. 11, 20) from Colossae; Zenas (Titus 3:13) from Crete; Tychicus (Acts 20:4) from Asia; Trophimus (Acts 20:4) from Ephesus; Epaphraditus (Phil. 4:18) from Philippi; Aristarcus, Secundas (Acts 20:4), and possibly Demas (Col. 4:14) from Thessalonica; Sophater (Acts 20:4) from Borea; Stephanus and Fortunatus (1 Cor. 16:17–18) and possibly Lucius (Rom. 16:21) from Corinth; Artemas (Titus 3:12) probably from Nicopolis; Crescens (2 Tim. 4:10) probably from Rome; and Titus, Erastus (2 Tim. 4:19), Silvanus (1 Peter 5:12), Jason (Rom. 16:21), and Tertius (Rom. 16:22) from unnamed locations. Other names mentioned in Romans 16 may represent other mobile personnel, but the detail is too sketchy to determine this for sure.

12. This principle was recognized by a number of the early Reformers. We find, for example, in the Church Order developed at the Synod of Dordt in 1619 the final article stating the following: "Article 86: These Articles, relating to the lawful order of the Church, have been so drafted and adopted by common consent, that they, if the profit of the Church demand otherwise, may and ought to be altered, augmented or diminished. . . ." in Hall and Hall, *Paradigms in Polity*, 184.

13. Examples may be found in Philippians 2:6–11, 1 Timothy 2:5–6 and 3:16.

14. While the council did not want to impose any "further burden" (Acts 15:28), it did proceed to ask everyone, Gentiles included, to "abstain from what has been sacrificed to idols and from blood and from what is strangled and from fornication" (29). The reason for these additional requirements would seem to lie in the desire of the council to achieve peace between Jewish and Gentile Christians by asking everyone to avoid those particular practices which would be most offensive to the Jew. While this represents an interesting twist on who is being asked to function as the stronger brother, it nevertheless represents a policy decision of trying to apply a confessional understanding of the gospel.

15. Filson, *A New Testament History*.

16. Brown, *The New International Dictionary of New Testament Theology*, vol. 3, 544–49.

17. Calvin, for example, takes this approach in his treatment of this passage. See John Calvin, *Sermons on the Epistle to the Ephesians* (Carlisle, Pa.: The Banner of Truth Trust, [1562] 1973), 361–75.

18. Kung, *The Church*, 410–13.

# Selected Bibliography

Ahlstrom, Sydney E. *A Religious History of the American People.* 2 vols. Garden City, N.Y.: Image Books, 1975.

Allen, Roland. *Missionary Methods: St. Paul's or Ours?* Grand Rapids: Eerdmans, (1927) 1962.

Anderson, Leith. *A Church for the 21st Century.* Minneapolis: Bethany House, 1992.

Arn, Win, ed. *The Pastor's Church Growth Handbook.* Pasadena, Calif.: Church Growth Press, 1979.

Barna, George. *User Friendly Churches.* Ventura, Calif.: Regal Books, 1991.

"Belgic Confession." *Psalter Hymnal.* Grand Rapids: CRC Publications, 1987.

Best, Steven and Douglas Kellner. *Postmodern Theory.* New York: Guilford Press, 1991.

Birkey, Del. *The House Church: A Model for Renewing the Church.* Scottdale, Pa.: Herald Press, 1988.

Blauw, Johannes. *The Missionary Nature of the Church.* Grand Rapids: Eerdmans, 1962.

Boer, Harry R. *Pentecost and Missions.* Grand Rapids: Eerdmans, 1961.

Boff, Leonardo. *Ecclesiogenesis: The Base Communities Reinvent the Church.* Maryknoll, N.Y.: Orbis, 1986.

Bosch, David J. *Transforming Mission: Paradigm Shifts in Theology of Mission.* Maryknoll, N.Y.: Orbis, 1991.

Bradley, Martin B. et al., eds. *Churches and Church Membership in the United States 1990.* Atlanta: Glenmary Research Center, 1992.

Brown, Colin, ed. *The New International Dictionary of New Testament Theology.* 3 vols. Grand Rapids: Zondervan, (1971) 1978.

Brown, Daniel A. *The Other Side of Pastoral Ministry.* Grand Rapids: Zondervan, 1996.

Selected Bibliography

Callahan, Kennon L. *Effective Church Leadership*. New York: Harper and Row, 1990.

Calvin, John. *Sermons on the Epistle to the Ephesians*. Carlisle, Pa.: The Banner of Truth Trust, (1562) 1973.

Carey, William. *An Enquiry into the Obligation of Christians to Use Means for the Conversion of the Heathens*. London: Hodder and Stoughton, 1792.

Carroll, Jackson W. et al., eds. *Handbook for Congregational Studies*. Nashville: Abingdon, 1986.

Clowney, Edmund P. *The Church: Contours of Christian Theology*. Downers Grove, Ill.: InterVarsity, 1995.

Commission on World Mission and Evangelism. "Mission and Evangelism: An Ecumenical Affirmation." *International Review of Mission* 71, no. 284 (October 1982): 427–51.

Conn, Harvie E. *Eternal Word and Changing World: Theology, Anthropology, and Mission in Trialogue*. Grand Rapids: Zondervan, Academie Books, 1984.

Connor, Steven. *Postmodernist Culture*. Cambridge, Mass.: Basil Blackwell, 1989.

Cook, Guillermo. *The Expectation of the Poor: Latin American Basic Ecclesial Communities in Protestant Perspective*. Maryknoll, N.Y.: Orbis, 1985.

Dempter, Murray A. et al. *Called and Empowered: Global Mission in Pentecostal Perspective*. Peabody, Mass.: Hendrickson, 1991.

Dulles, Avery. *Models of the Church*. New York: Doubleday, Image Books, 1974 (1987).

Filson, F. *A New Testament History*. London: SCM, 1965.

Frazier, E. Franklin. *The Negro Church in America*. New York: Schocken, 1974.

George, Carl F. *Prepare Your Church for the Future*. Tarrytown, N.Y.: Fleming H. Revell, 1991.

Gerber, Virgil. *A Manual for Evangelism/Church Growth*. South Pasadena, Calif.: Wm. Carey Library, 1973.

Getz, Gene A. *Sharpening the Focus of the Church*. Chicago: Moody, 1974.

Giles, Kevin. *What on Earth Is the Church?* Downers Grove, Ill.: InterVarsity, 1995.

Grant, John Webster. *The Church in the Canadian Era*. Toronto, Ontario: McGraw-Hill Ryerson Ltd., 1972.

Grenz, Stanley J. *A Primer on Postmodernism*. Grand Rapids: Eerdmans, 1996.

Guder, Darrell L., ed. *Missional Church: A Theological Vision for the Sending of the Church in North America*. Grand Rapids: Eerdmans, 1998.

Hall, David W. and Hall, Joseph H., eds. *Paradigms in Polity*. Grand Rapids: Eerdmans, 1994.

Hauerwas, Stanley and William H. Willimon. *Resident Aliens*. Nashville: Abingdon, 1989.

Hiebert, Paul G. "Critical Contextualization." *International Bulletin of Missionary Research* 11, no. 3 (July 1987): 104–12.

Hodges, Melvin L. *The Indigenous Church*. Springfield, Mo.: Gospel Publishing House, 1953.

Hodgson, Peter C. *Revisioning the Church*. Minneapolis: Fortress, 1988.

Hoekendijk, J. C. *The Church Inside Out*. Philadelphia: Westminster, 1964.

Hoge, Dean R. and David A. Roozen, eds. *Understanding Church Growth and Decline 1950–1978*. New York: Pilgrim, 1979.

Hogg, William Richey. *Ecumenical Foundations*. New York: Harper and Brothers, 1952.

Hollinger, Robert. *Postmodernism and the Social Sciences*. Thousand Oaks, Calif.: Sage Publications, 1994.

Hudson, Winthrop S. *Religion in America*. New York: Charles Scribner's Sons, 1965.

Hunsberger, George R. and Craig Van Gelder. *The Church Between Gospel and Culture: The Emerging Mission in North America*. Grand Rapids: Eerdmans, 1996.

Hunter, George G. III. *Church for the Unchurched*. Nashville: Abingdon, 1996.

Kennedy, D. James. *Evangelism Explosion*. Wheaton: Tyndale, 1970.

Kung, Hans. *The Church*. New York: Sheed and Ward, 1967.

Ladd, George Eldon. *A Theology of the New Testament*. Grand Rapids: Eerdmans, 1974.

Lausanne Committee for World Evangelization. "No. 21: Grand Rapids Report—Evangelism and Social Responsibility, An Evangelical Commitment." *Lausanne Occasional Papers*. Lausanne Committee for World Evangelization and World Evangelical Fellowship, 1982.

Leith, John H., ed. *Creeds and Confessions*. Richmond: John Knox, 1973.

Lewis, A. T. *Zinzendorf the Ecumenical Pioneer*. London: SCM, 1962.

Locke, John. "A Letter Concerning Toleration." Edited by Maurice Cranston. *Locke on Politics, Religion, and Education*. New York: Collier, 1965.

Mains, David R. *Full Circle*. Waco: Word, 1971.

Marty, Martin E. *Righteous Empire*. New York: Dial Press, 1970.

McGavran, Donald A. *Understanding Church Growth*. Grand Rapids: Eerdmans, 1970.

McNeill, John T. *The History and Character of Calvinism*. New York: Oxford University Press, 1954.

Selected Bibliography

Mead, Frank S. *Handbook of Denominations in the United States.* Revised by Samuel S. Hill. 9th ed. Nashville: Abingdon, 1990.

Middleton, J. Richard and Brian J. Walsh. *Truth Is Stranger Than It Used to Be.* Downers Grove, Ill.: InterVarsity, 1995.

Minear, Paul S. *Images of the Church in the New Testament.* Philadelphia: Westminster, 1960.

Moltmann, Jurgen. *The Church in the Power of the Spirit.* Minneapolis: Fortress, (1975) 1993.

Mullin, Robert B. and Richey, Russell E., eds. *Reimagining Denominationalism.* New York: Oxford University Press, 1994.

Neill, Steven. *A History of Christian Missions.* New York: Penguin, 1964.

Nevius, John L. *The Planting and Development of Missionary Churches.* Nutley, N.J.: Presbyterian and Reformed Publishing Co., (1886) 1958.

Niebuhr, H. Richard. *Christ and Culture.* New York: Harper, 1951.

Newbigin, Lesslie. *One Body, One Gospel, One World.* London and New York: International Missionary Council, 1958.

———. *The Open Secret.* Grand Rapids: Eerdmans, 1978.

———. *Foolishness to the Greeks.* Grand Rapids: Eerdmans, 1986.

Ogden, Greg. *The New Reformation: Returning the Ministry to the People of God.* Grand Rapids: Zondervan, 1990.

Parvin, Earl. *Missions USA.* Chicago: Moody, 1985.

Piet, John H. *The Road Ahead: A Theology for the Church in Mission.* Grand Rapids: Eerdmans, 1970.

Richards, Lawrence O. *A New Face for the Church.* Grand Rapids: Zondervan, 1970.

Richey, Russell E. *Denominationalism.* Nashville: Abingdon, 1977.

Ridderbos, Herman. *The Coming of the Kingdom.* Philadelphia: Presbyterian and Reformed Publishing Co., 1962.

Roozen, David A. and C. Kirk Hadaway. *Church and Denominational Growth.* Nashville: Abingdon, 1993.

Schaller, Lyle E. *The Seven-Day-a-Week Church.* Nashville: Abingdon, 1992.

Senior, Donald and Carroll Stuhlmueller. *The Biblical Foundations for Mission.* Maryknoll, N.Y.: Orbis, 1983.

Sanneh, Lamin. *Translating the Message: The Missionary Impact on Culture.* Maryknoll, N.Y.: Orbis, 1993.

Shawchuck, Norman and Roger Heuser. *Leading the Congregation.* Nashville: Abingdon, 1993.

Shawchuck, Norman and Gustave Rath. *Benchmarks of Quality in the Church.* Nashville: Abingdon, 1994.

Smelser, Neil J. *Handbook of Sociology*. Newbury Park, Calif.: Sage Publications, 1988.

Smith, Ebbie C. *Balanced Church Growth*. Nashville: Broadman, 1984.

Snyder, Howard A. *Models of the Kingdom*. Nashville: Abingdon, 1991.

Trueheart, Charles. "Welcome to the Next Church." *The Atlantic Monthly*, August 1996, 37–58.

van der Ven, Johannes A. *Ecclesiology in Context*. Grand Rapids: Eerdmans, (1993) 1996.

Van Engen, Charles. *God's Missionary People*. Grand Rapids: Baker, 1991.

———. *Mission on the Way*. Grand Rapids: Baker, 1996.

Van Gelder, Craig. "Missional Challenge: Understanding the Church in North America." In *Missional Church: A Theological Vision for the Sending of the Church in North America*, edited by Darrell L. Guder. Grand Rapids: Eerdmans, 1998.

Verkuyl, J. *Contemporary Missiology: An Introduction*. Grand Rapids: Eerdmans, 1978.

Wagner, C. Peter. *Strategies for Church Growth*. Ventura, Calif.: Regal Books, 1987.

Warren, Rick. *The Purpose Driven Church*. Grand Rapids: Zondervan, 1995.

Whiteman, Darrell L. "Contextualization: The Theory, the Gap, the Challenge." *International Bulletin of Missionary Research* 21, no. 1 (January 1997): 2–7.

Winter, Ralph D. "The Two Structures of God's Redemptive Mission." *Missiology: An International Review* 2, no. 1 (January 1974): 121–39.

Wuthnow, Robert. *The Restructuring of American Religion*. Princeton, N.J.: Princeton University Press, 1988.

Selected Bibliography

# Index

Advocate-Helper, 86–87, 142–43
already/not yet, 33, 75, 79–81, 82, 96–98, 103, 111, 113, 120, 133, 139–40
Anderson, Wilhelm, 33
Anglican-Episcopal, 123
Apostles' Creed, 50, 54–55, 111
assembly
  for accountability, 179
  and connectional processes, 172–73
  for decision making, 179
*Atlantic Monthly, The*, 23–24
attributes of the church
  apostolic, 50–52, 54–55, 65, 114–16, 123–26, 145
  catholic, 41, 49–51, 55–56, 106, 114–16, 118–20, 123, 160
  communion of the saints, 50–52, 54, 111
  discipline, 54
  five, 50
  holy, 50–52, 55–56, 106, 114–16, 123
  and ministry of the church, 51
  and nature of the church, 51, 116–18, 159
  and Nicene Creed, 51, 54, 114–16, 118, 123
  one, 50–51, 55–56, 106, 114–16, 121–22
  and organization of the church, 52
  *See also* Apostles' Creed; Augsburg Confession; Belgic Confession; nature of the church; visible church
Augsburg Confession, 54
Augustine, 56

baptism
  of the Holy Spirit, 78–80
  with fire, 78–81
  *See also* marks; sacraments

*basileia*, 75
Belgic Confession, 54, 143
believers, priesthood of, 58, 131
biblical images of the church
  the body of Christ, 110–11
  the communion of saints, 50–51, 96, 111–12
  core, 107–13
  the creation of the spirit, 112–13
  and ministry of the church, 107
  and nature of the church, 107
  and organization of the church, 107
  the people of God, 108–9
bishop(s)
  of the church, 50, 120, 123
  office of, 51, 55, 115
  role of, 69
body of Christ, 110–11
Brethren of Common Life, 61

Calvin, John, 53
Canada, church in, 15, 43
  *See also* denominations
Carey, William, 29, 62, 64
catholic, defined, 49
  *See also* attributes of the church
Christian Church (Disciples of Christ), 69
Christology
  controversy, 50
  and the Trinity, 129–30
church
  anticipated by Jesus, 84–88
  balance, 159
  and biblical foundations, 44
  black, 70, 72
  contextual, 118–19, 144, 159–60, 166
  and cultural setting, 43–44

Index

redemptive reign, 73–100, 139
  God's, 33, 76–80, 82–83, 87, 95,
    108–9, 125, 130, 132, 160–61, 164
  implemented, 103–4
  introduced, 102
  and the kingdom, 74–75, 95
  and ministry of the church, 74,
    88–89
  and nature of the church, 74, 88–89
  and organization of the church, 74,
    88–89
  and the strong man, 133
Reformation, 61, 112 121, 129–31, 159
Reformers, 52–55, 123, 142–43
Roman Catholic Church
  and attributes of the church, 52–52,
    54, 57, 123
  and Latin America, 33–34
  and papacy, 54–55
  and perceived abuses, 129, 142
  and Pope Paul VI, 34
  and social community, 115
  and Vatican II, 33–34

sacraments
  baptism, 55, 77, 148–49
  Lord's Supper, 55, 110, 129, 131,
    148–49
  See also grace; marks, three; marks,
    two
salvation, individualistic, 131
  See also pietism
Scottish Presbyterians, 66
seed. See sin and redemption
sentness, 125
serving, 153
sin and redemption, 76, 93–96, 103
  See also evil
social
  community, 51, 59, 60, 71, 75, 92, 96,
    107, 110–12, 115–17, 128, 136,
    153, 161, 166, 175
  fellowship, 108
  meaning of, 25
  organization, 67, 71–72, 104
  reality of, 146
social-contract theory, 67, 69
social sciences
  and ministry of the church, 24

  and nature of the church, 24
  and organization of the church, 24
Spener, Philipp Jacob, 62
Spirit's work
  and church organization, 157, 160,
    180
  and corporate faith, 145–46
  and corporate life, 143–44
  and fellowship, 152–53
  and gifts, 145
  and leading and teaching, 142, 162
  See also work
stewardship, 86, 91–92, 124, 154
strong man. See redemptive reign
structure
  connectional, 59, 156–84
  mobile, 173–74, 176, 179
  See also organization
suffering servant, 76
synagogue, 105

teaching. See Sprit's work
temple
  in Jerusalem, 103
  spiritual, 104
Trinity
  character of, 96–97, 122
  ministry of the, 139
  mission of the, 33, 97, 128
  understanding of the, 35
  See also work
Twelve, the
  and authority, 123
  and the church, 85–86, 123–25
  and forming the church, 124–25
  as foundation of the church, 84
  as a little flock, 84–86, 133
  and the Spirit, 86–87

unity. See government; nature of the
  church

variety. See New Testament church
visible church, the, 106–7, 115
  as apostolic, 123–26
  as catholic, 118–20
  and confessions, 56
  diversity of, 165–72
  as holy, 116–18

206

Index

Craig Van Gelder is professor of congregational mission at Luther Seminary in St. Paul, Minnesota, where he resides. Previously he taught at Calvin Theological Seminary as professor of domestic missiology. He holds a doctorate in missions from Southwestern Baptist Theological Seminary and a doctorate in administration in urban affairs from the University of Texas at Arlington. He is general editor of the Gospel and Our Culture series, in which he coedited *The Church Between Gospel and Culture,* and is editor of *Confident Witness—Changing World.* He regularly consults with churchs, serving as senior associate consultant with Church Innovations Institute.